Perfect OUTDOOR GRILL

101 Outdoor Grill Recipes Plus How To Tips & Illustrated Instructions!

By Matt Jason

healthy happy Foodie

HHF Press

San Francisco

COPYRIGHT © 2020 Healthy Happy Foodie Press (HHF Press)

First published 2020

All rights reserved. No part of this book may be reproduced in any form or by any electronic or mechanical means, including information storage and retrieval systems, without permission in writing from the publisher, except by reviewers, who may quote brief passages in a review.

Editor: HHF Press

Art Direction: HHF Press

Illustrations: HHF Press

All photographs in this book © HHF Press, © Shutterstock.com or © Depositphotos.com

Published in the United States of America by HHF Press

268 Bush St, #3042

San Francisco, CA 94104 USA

www.HHFPress.com

Disclaimer:

Although the publisher and authors of this book are practically obsessed with modern cooking techniques, neither the publisher nor the authors represent or are affiliated with any of the brands mentioned in this text.

All content herein represents the authors' own experiences and opinions, and do not represent medical or health advice. The responsibility for the consequences of your actions, including your use or misuse of any suggestion or procedure described in this book lies not with the authors, publisher or distributors of this book. We recommend using common sense and consulting with a licensed health professional before changing your diet or exercise. The authors or the publisher do not assume any liability for the use of or inability to use any or all of the information contained in this book, nor do the authors or publisher accept responsibility for any type of loss or damage that may be experienced by the user as the result of activities occurring from the use of any information in this book. Use the information responsibly and at your own risk.

The authors and publisher reserve the right to make changes he or she deems required to future versions of the publication to maintain accuracy.

REVIEWS

"

By the looks of the instructions it looks simple and easy to use. I liked the illustrated instructions and quick start chapter!

Sabrina S.

"

After some grill basics, such as how to use the various buttons and controls, I was surprised to find some "pro tips" I hadn't thought of, and a ton of recipes that look appetizing and fun. Nice collection!

Camilla V.

"

For an outdoor grill junkie like me, I found this book to have some fantastic recipes! I also really appreciated the 10 Minute fast start chapter — it should be in the actual manual from the manufacturer.

Gilly A.

"

This book came as a gift with my new grill. I quickly realized it's not from the manufacturer, but I like it better because it seems more straightforward and, dare I say, more useful than the guide that came with the grill. The recipes cover a lot of territory...I'm pleasantly surprised.

Dave B.

"

Wow, this book came in handy! I had to prepare for a big BBQ party and I found some excellent ideas that made the party a huge success. Consider the recipes for sandwiches and desserts, they're pretty amazing actually. Who would have thought of making a peach and berry pizza on a grill? It's amazing!

Armand S.

INTRODUCTION

WHO THIS BOOK IS FOR?

If you have just purchased, or already own, a gas grill, then you need this book! Here's why:

GET THE MOST OUT OF YOUR GAS GRILL!

Illustrated instructions, a quick start guide and beyond-the-manual tips and tricks will teach you how to get the most out of your grill so that it becomes your family's favorite way to cook outdoors.

GET A FAST START WITH "10 MINUTE QUICK-START!"

Our illustrated "10 Minute Quick-Start" chapter will walk you through your first complete meals in under 10 minutes, so you can quickly enjoy delicious burgers, steaks, vegetables, and more instead of spending all of your time reading instruction manuals.

CLEAR, ILLUSTRATED INSTRUCTIONS.

We'll make using a gas grill so simple you can start cooking in minutes while avoiding beginner mistakes such as wrong heat, wrong ingredients, food sticking to the grill, etc.

GO BEYOND THE INSTRUCTION MANUAL.

Our Pro tips will have you cooking like the pro's in no time. Learn the science behind perfectly grilled food so that you can confidently make the best, most nutritious outdoor meals you've ever had.

UNBIASED RECOMMENDATIONS, WORKAROUNDS, AND PRO TIPS.

To help you confidently make amazing meals that are perfectly tailored to your family, while avoiding common mistakes, wherever you go!

ALL THE RECIPES YOU'LL EVER NEED!

101 of the best recipes on the planet will allow you to make the classic BBQs, lunches, and dinners you are already familiar with, as well as fun and exciting recipes which will give your family the variety they love.

CONTENTS

- 1 ABOUT YOUR GAS GRILL
- 7 HOW TO USE A GAS GRILL
- 12 10 MINUTE QUICK-START
- 15 PRO TIPS
- 21 **MAIN DISHES: POULTRY**
  - 22 Sweet orange Chili Lime Chicken
  - 23 Zesty Chili Lime Chicken
  - 25 Classic BBQ Chicken
  - 26 Chipotle Adobe Chicken
  - 27 Honey Balsamic Marinated Chicken
  - 28 California Grilled Chicken
  - 29 Salsa Verde Marinated Chicken
  - 30 Chicken Wings With Sweet Red Chili and Peach Glaze
  - 32 Hawaiian Chicken Skewers
  - 33 Chicken Tacos With Avocado Crema
  - 34 Kale Caesar Salad With Grilled Chicken
  - 35 Hasselback Stuffed Chicken
  - 37 Fiery Italian Chicken Skewers
  - 38 Creole Chicken Stuffed With Cheese & Peppers
  - 39 Teriyaki Chicken And Veggie Rice Bowls
  - 40 Yellow Curry Chicken Wings
  - 41 Korean Grilled Chicken Wings With Scallion
  - 42 Buffalo Grilled Chicken Wings
  - 44 Poppyseed Chicken Summer Salad
  - 45 Lemon Ginger Chicken With Fruit Salsa
  - 46 Lemon-Olive Grilled Chicken
  - 47 Chicken Thighs With Ginger-Sesame Glaze
  - 48 Soba Noodle Chicken with Miso Vinaigrette
  - 49 Chicken Satay with Almond Butter Sauce
  - 50 Tequila-Glazed Grilled Chicken Thighs
  - 51 Root Beer Can Chicken
  - 52 Basil, Blackberry, And Grilled Chicken Salad
  - 53 Honey Sriracha Grilled Chicken Thighs
- 55 **MAIN DISHES: BEEF**
  - 56 Caprese Flank Steak
  - 57 Tender Steak with Pineapple Rice
  - 59 Rib-Eye Steak with Herbed Steak Butter
  - 60 High-Low Strip Steak
  - 61 Greek Flank Steak Gyros
  - 62 Coffee and Brown Sugar-Crusted Skirt Steak with Grilled Okra and Jalapeños
  - 63 Coffee-Rubbed Texas-Style Brisket
  - 64 Mexican Grilled Steak Salad
  - 66 Grilled Steaks with Sweet-Spicy Hoisin Sauce
  - 67 Greek Feta & Spinach Burgers
  - 69 Tuscan-Style Steak with Crispy Potatoes
  - 70 Caprese Grilled Filet Mignon
  - 71 Flank Steak with Garlic and Rosemary
  - 72 Beef Pinwheels
  - 73 Carne Asada
  - 74 Basic Juicy NY Strip Steak
  - 76 Rib Eye Steak with Romaine Marmalade and Watercress
  - 77 Flash-Marinated Skirt Steak
- 79 **MAIN DISHES: PORK**
  - 80 Sticky-Sweet Pork Shoulder
  - 81 Pineapple Bacon Pork Chops
  - 83 Habanero-Marinated Pork Chops
  - 84 Moroccan Spiced Pork Tenderloin with Creamy Harissa Sauce
  - 85 Pork Tenderloin Sandwiches
  - 86 Sweet & Spicy BBQ Ribs
  - 87 Herb-Crusted Mediterranean Pork Tenderloin
  - 88 Grilled Pork Chops with Herb Apple Compote
  - 90 Dijon Honey Pork Chops with Tomato-Peach Salad

- 91 Honey Soy Pork Chops
- 92 Sweet Heat Cheerwine Baby Back Ribs
- 93 Big John's Chili-Rubbed Ribs
- 95 Glazed Country Ribs
- 96 Yucatan-Style Grilled Pork
- 97 Sweet Smoked Pork Ribs

99 MAIN DISHES: SEAFOOD

- 100 Gremolata Swordfish Skewers
- 101 Spiced Snapper with Mango and Red Onion Salad
- 102 Grilled Oysters with Spiced Tequila Butter
- 104 Scallops with Lemony Salsa Verde
- 105 Spicy Grilled Squid
- 107 Spiced Crab Legs
- 108 Basted Dungeness Crab
- 109 Pop-Open Clams with Horseradish-Tabasco Sauce
- 110 Clam Toasts with Lemon and Green Olives
- 111 Potato Shrimp Foil Packets
- 112 Honey-Lime Tilapia and Corn Foil Pack
- 113 Pistachio-Lemon Pesto Shrimp
- 114 Mexican Shrimp Tacos
- 116 Flaky Grilled Halibut
- 117 Spicy Grilled Jumbo Shrimp
- 118 Lobster Tails with Lime Basil Butter
- 119 Coconut Pineapple Shrimp Skewers
- 121 Salmon Fillets with Basil Butter & Broccolini
- 122 Halibut Fillets with Spinach and Olives
- 123 Sweet-and-Smoky Cedar-Planked Salmon

125 BURGERS

- 126 Juicy Lucy Burger
- 127 Breakfast Burger
- 128 Black Forest Burger
- 129 Pizza Burger
- 130 Texas Chili Burger
- 131 Balsamic Portobello Burger
- 132 Spiced Turkey Burger
- 133 Salmon Burgers
- 134 California Burger
- 135 Sauteed Mushroom Burger
- 136 BLT Burger
- 137 Taco Burger
- 138 Gorgonzola Lamb Burger
- 139 Eggplant Caprese Burger
- 140 BCO Burger
- 141 Rueben Burger

143 SANDWICHES & BREADS

- 144 Cheesy Ham and Pineapple Sandwich
- 145 Garlic Parmesan Grilled Cheese Sandwiches
- 146 Grilled Veggie Panini
- 148 Grilled Pizza Cheese
- 149 Turkey Pesto Panini
- 150 Greek Chicken Salad Pita Pockets
- 151 Mini Portobello Burgers
- 152 Layered Beef & Corn Burger
- 153 Prosciutto Pesto Hot Dog
- 154 Curry Pork Wraps With Nectarine Chutney
- 155 Sun-Dried Tomato and Chicken Flatbreads
- 157 Bacon Jalapeno Wraps
- 158 Veggie Pesto Flatbread
- 159 Grilled Vegetable Pizza
- 160 Cornbread with Jalapeño Honey Butter
- 161 Charred Bread with Ricotta and Cherry Salsa

163 SAUCES AND MARINADES

- 164 Classic Kansas City BBQ Sauce
- 165 Savory Chinese Marinade
- 166 Thai Chili Sauce
- 167 Carolina Gold BBQ Sauce
- 168 Jerk Rub
- 169 Peruvian Chicken Marinade
- 170 Teriyaki Sauce

CHAPTER 1

ABOUT YOUR GAS GRILL

WHAT DOES IT DO?

Most gas grills provides about 500 inches of professional grade grill for your back yard or really anywhere you go. Now, you can make professional quality meals and get the same results professional chefs achieve every time you cook. Make steaks, burgers, poultry, vegetables, and so much more. A gas grill is designed to produce perfectly even and adjustable heat over different cooking zones, so you can always have the exact temperature you need at a moment's notice.

Your gas grill is made with professional grade materials and provides professional quality heat. This means you can carefully control everything you cook with individual controls for each zone. Vegetables don't cook properly at the same temperature as a steak, and a gas grill allows you to cook both, perfectly, at the same time.

A gas grill takes backyard grilling to the next level with the addition of a thermometer which allows you to easily control the temperature inside your grill at all times. As a result, you can use your grill to cook foods like brisket and ribs, which benefit from low and slow cooking.

Because it is built from industrial grade materials, your gas grill will be a versatile appliance for many years to come. The burners are made from stainless steel and are guaranteed to produce perfectly even and powerful heat. A stainless steel warming rack allows you to keep already cooked foods warm, which gives you even more flexibility.

Say goodbye to dirty charcoal and matches forever. Charcoal is dirty, expensive, and harmful to your health, so why are you still using it? A gas grill uses a standard refillable propane take which attaches to the grill with

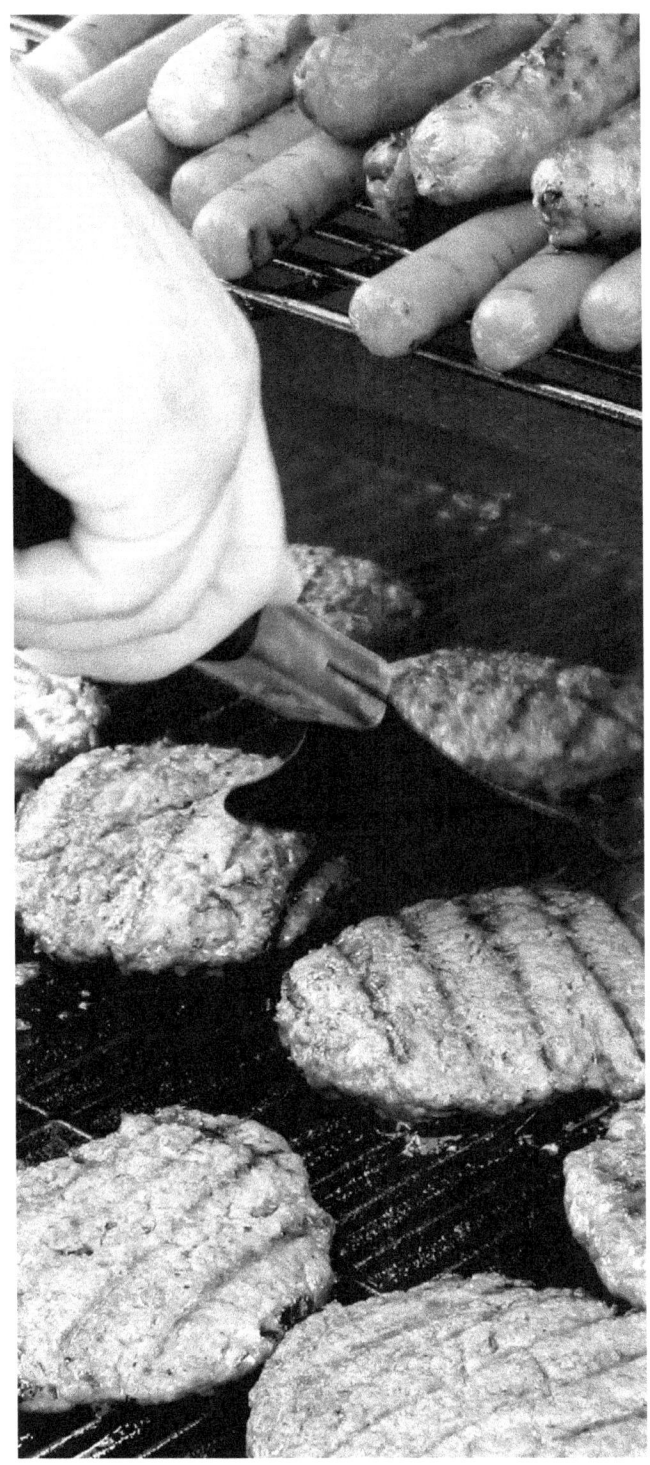

ease. And thanks to the simple push button igniter, starting your grill is as easy as pushing a button.

WHO IS IT GOOD FOR?

Because a gas grill is large enough to cook all the parts of a complete meal at the same time, it is perfect for families who love perfectly prepared backyard favorites like burgers, steaks, and veggies, many grills also feature a side burner which is perfect for those who also want the convenience of a more conventional stove burner to cook things like eggs or sauces while grilling.

Do you love to cook big meals on the go? A gas grill is perfect for camping and tailgating because of how easy it is to transport and set up. Pack it up for your next camping trip and set it up when you want to make an amazing outdoor meal. A grill is also perfect for anyone who loves making fresh grilled food for a professional tailgate party. Since the grill easily fits in the trunk of a car, you can take it with you to the game and set it up in minutes. Impress the whole parking lot with the amazing food you make for your fellow fans.

WHO IS IT NOT GOOD FOR?

Everyone loves food cooked in the open air, but if you don't have a large enough outdoor space in which to use a gas grill, this may not be for you. A good rule of thumb is that you can use the grill anywhere you would use a charcoal grill.

A FEW CAUTIONS

Because a gas grill uses an external propane tank, you will want to exercise caution while connecting and disconnecting the tank. Always make sure all connection points are clean and free of debris. When attaching the hose to the tank, make sure the valve is completely tightened before allowing gas to flow to the grill.

A gas grill's powerful burners produce amazing results, but because they get very hot, you should make sure children are always supervised when near the grill.

WHAT ARE ITS HEALTH BENEFITS?

Charcoal grilling has been the standard for many years, but it carries a whole host of risks. First of all, charcoal fires increase the risk of fires in your yard. That's pretty bad, but did you know that cooking with charcoal also increases your risk of cancer? The combination of charcoal, lighter fluid, and dripping fats causes a variety of compounds that are considered carcinogenic. And you're not just breathing these chemicals when you cook. They're actually coating your food! Charcoal grills also contribute to air pollution by releasing large amounts of carbon monoxide and carbon dioxide into the atmosphere. A gas grill, on the other hand, uses no charcoal and is much safer to use.

A BRIEF HISTORY OF GRILLING

You may not be surprised to hear that grilling food is a pretty old technique. In fact, it goes back over a half a million years. Early humans found that meat cooked over fire was actually more nutritious than raw meat. The reason? Bioavailability. In short, cooking meat changes the structure of proteins and fats, allowing them to be more efficiently digested and absorbed by the body. Until the 1940s grilling was mostly something that people did around campfires, but after World War II and the expansion of suburbs, the popularity of backyard grilling skyrocketed. By the 1950s the back yard BBQ was a staple of family entertaining, and it remains this way today.

MORE EVEN HEAT THAN CHARCOAL

One of the amazing features of a gas grill is that you have so much control over the heat. Old fashioned charcoal grills offer a lot of heat, but it doesn't last long, and you don't have much control over it. You have to estimate how much charcoal you will need to produce the right amount of heat, but you never really know if it's going to be right. And you also don't have much control over where the heat is. With a gas grill, you get four independently controlled burners for maximum flexibility and guaranteed even heat.

THE WORLD'S BEST FLAVOR BARS

Sure, cooking over an open flame imparts great flavor, but what really kicks it up a notch are the specially designed flavor bars which translate dripping fats into pure smoky flavor. The triangular shaped bars sit across the burners and wait for juices from meats to drip into the grill. As soon as the juices hit the flavor bars, they are immediately vaporized and float back up to season your food. This gives you all the smoky flavor you expect from grilling without using unhealthy charcoal.

CHAPTER 2
HOW TO USE A GAS GRILL

SETTING UP THE GRILL

Once you have removed a gas grill from its packaging, be sure to consult the user manual to ensure you have all of the included parts and fasteners.

Follow the step-by-step instructions to assemble the grill, and makes sure to place it on a level surface so that it cannot roll.

Once you have fully assembled the grill, you can use the valve hose to attach a canister of propane.

LEARNING THE CONTROLS

A gas grill has easy to use controls that will have you cooking in no time.

1. **IGNITION BUTTON:**
The battery controlled ignition button lights your griddle.
Simply press, hold, and the left most burner will light.

2. **LEFT BURNER KNOB:**
Turn clockwise to control the heat on the left burner.

3. **LEFT-CENTER BURNER KNOB:**
Turn clockwise to increase the heat on the left-center burner.

4. **RIGHT-CENTER BURNER KNOB:**
Turn clockwise to increase the heat on the right-center burner.

5. **RIGHT BURNER KNOB:**
Turn clockwise to increase the heat on the right burner.

6. **LEFT SIDE BURNER KNOB:**
Turn clockwise to increase the heat on the burner.

THE GRILLING PROCESS

Thanks to a gas grill you can make almost anything with amazing results. Because the grill has four independent burners, you are free to cook different foods at different temperatures at the same time. Unlike charcoal grills, this gives you far greater flexibility with one appliance. And thanks to the lid-mounted thermometer, you can easily keep track of how hot your grill is at all times. This makes adjusting the heat as easy as can be.

When you first light the grill, you will need to wait a few minutes before cooking. A gas grill features cooking grates which are easy to clean and are rust resistant. Because they are cast iron, however, they will take a few minutes to heat up. Allowing them to reach the proper temperature will also help prevent food from sticking during cooking.

WORKAROUNDS

A gas grill features an easy to use ignition system, but if you find that the ignition burner is not lighting there are several possible causes. First, check to see if the battery in the igniter has enough power. If that is not the problem, make sure you have enough gas in the propane tank. Another problem may be a clogged burner or gas jet. Because food or other debris can fall into the burners, they may become clogged over time. If this is the case, remove the grates and flavor bars and use a damp sponge to clean out the burners or gas jets.

A gas grill features a drip drawer which allows for grease to collect without dripping on your patio or yard. During cooking, grease is channeled to a small collection pan located underneath the grill. If cooking debris falls into the channel it can become clogged and the grease may overflow instead of finding its way to the drip drawer. To avoid this, simply check the channel periodically to make sure that it has not become clogged. Wiping it out with a damp cloth or paper towel every so often will ensure the cleanest possible grilling experience.

A gas grill is already quite portable, but to add even more flexibility, you can use a small propane tank. To use the grill with either a one or five pound tank, you can purchase fitting adapters that will allow you to use a smaller tank. Just make sure you've purchased the correct size before using.

10 Minute Quick-Start

LET'S GET STARTED!

Since your gas grill has four individual burners you can cook a complete mixed grill all at once. This is perfect for camping or for a festive summertime dinner for the whole family. We're going to start with classic surf and turf skewers, which are sure to delight the entire family. In fact, it'll probably smell so good, the neighbors might just want to drop by.

1 COLLECT THESE INGREDIENTS

- 2 lb. top sirloin, cut into large chunks
- 2 lb. jumbo shrimp, cleaned
- 2 yellow onions, cut into large chunks
- 2 green bell peppers, cut into chunks
- 2 yellow bell peppers, cut into chunks
- 2 red bell peppers, cut into chunks
- 1 lb. large white or portobello mushrooms
- Olive oil
- Salt and black pepper

2 COLLECT THESE TOOLS

- Chef's knife
- Bamboo skewers
- Grilling tongs
- Long handled basting brush
- Instant read thermometer

PERFECT OUTDOOR GRILL

The goal of "10 Minute Quick-Start" is to walk you through making your first meal so you "learn by doing" in under 10 minutes. Once you've had a chance to get familiar with how your grill works, you can begin experimenting with all different types of foods.

3 FOLLOW THESE INSTRUCTIONS

1. Light the gas grill and turn two of the burners to high heat, and two burners to medium heat.

2. Place the chunks of beef and shrimp on different skewers. Alternate the vegetables on their own skewers until you have used all of your ingredients.

3. Brush all of the skewers with olive oil and season with salt and black pepper.

4. First, place all of the beef skewers on the high heat part of the grill. Then, place the vegetable skewers on the medium heat area. Allow the beef skewers to cook for five minutes before flipping. Flip the vegetable skewers as needed to avoid them charring too much.

5. When three minutes remain, add the shrimp skewers to the medium heat area and cook one and a half minutes per side.

6. When all of the skewers have finished cooking, remove them from the grill and allow to rest for a few minutes before serving. You may serve with everything on the skewers or remove everything from the skewers and serve in large serving dishes.

CONGRATULATIONS!

You now have a perfectly cooked mixed grill for the whole family, and you have learned the basics of how to use a gas grill!

CHAPTER 3
PRO TIPS

BURN OFF CHEMICALS BEFORE FIRST USE

Prior to using your grill the first time, we recommend doing a pre-use season that will prepare the entire grill for use. Since protective coatings and paint can be used in the production of gas grills, you will want to light your grill and turn it up to high heat with the lid closed for about fifteen minutes before cooking for the first time. This will give the grill a chance to rid itself of any excess chemicals that may have been used in production. The result will be a clean grill, ready to use.

SEASON THE GRILL BEFORE USING

Unlike cast iron pans that need to be continuously seasoned to maintain a non-stick cooking surface, your gas grill only requires that the cooking grates be seasoned occasionally. To easily create a non-stick cooking surface, you only need a long handled grilling brush, some oil with a high smoke point, and a few paper towels. We recommend either vegetable oil or Canola oil for this because it won't leave behind any residual flavor. In addition to creating a non-stick cooking surface, this process will also protect your grilling grates against rust. In order to properly season the grates, brush a thin coating of oil onto the grates and then rub with paper towels until it is evenly distributed. Turn all of the burners on low heat and wait until the grates just start smoking. Wipe away any excess oil and repeat this step two to three more times. When cleaning the grates, avoid harsh detergents when possible, as this will eat away at the seasoning you have developed. Instead, try to clean the grates with hot water and a grill brush to remove cooked on pieces of food.

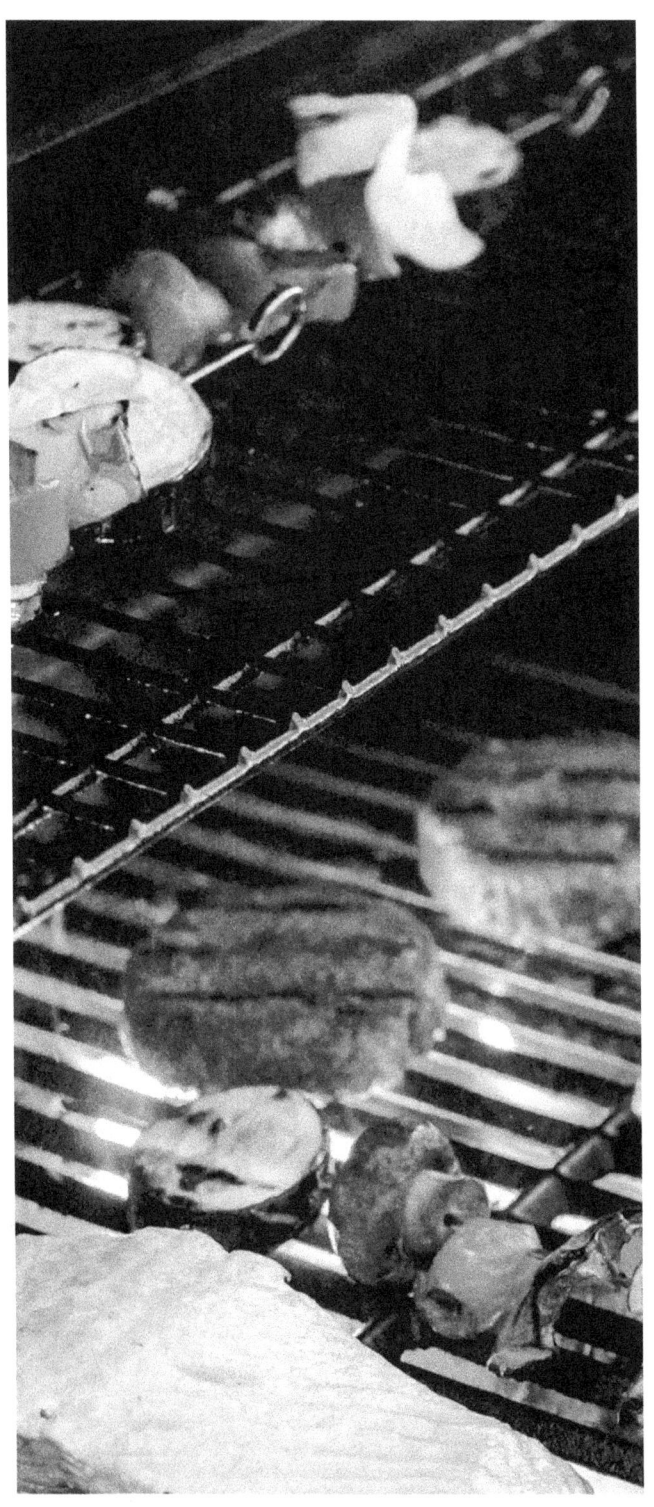

KEEP YOUR GRILL WORKING FROM SEASON TO SEASON

Because you are most likely going to keep your grill outside, you will need to make sure to do a few things before you store it and before you use it again after being stored. Before you store, make sure to disconnect the fuel tank and store away from the grill with a cap on the valve. You can also purchase a cover for the grill to keep out insects and dust. When you are ready to start using your grill again, make sure to check the burner area for spider webs. Webs are flammable and can cause flare ups if you do not clean them out before cooking. Check the level in your gas tank to make sure you have enough fuel to start cooking. Once the tank is attached and you are ready to cook, it's a good idea to perform a new season on the cooking surface. Simply follow the instructions above and your grill will be good as new.

INVEST IN THE PROPER TOOLS

Since a gas grill is a professional grade piece of equipment, you should have professional grade cooking tools to get the most out of it. While you may have an array of spatulas in the kitchen, to get the best out of your grill, we recommend buying a long metal spatula as well as long handled tongs and a long handled grill brush. Long handles mean less reaching, which mean less chance of getting burned. Grill spatulas are thin and flexible so you can scoop up things like burgers or chicken breast without dropping them. While there are many different types of tongs on the market, we recommend tongs with a wide end, which will make lifting things like steaks and chops much easier.

MARINATE FOR ADDED FLAVOR AND BETTER TEXTURE

Grilling adds so much delicious flavor that you just can't get from stove top cooking, and you can enhance these flavors by using marinades. Marinades are also a great way to tenderize meat while adding flavor. Chicken breasts are a grilling favorite, but they can become dry and bland if cooked plain. You can improve the texture of your chicken by using a very simple marinade consisting of olive oil, lime or lemon juice, salt, and pepper. The salt and pepper will add seasoning, while the acid in the citrus will tenderize and flavor the meat for a much more delicate texture. A simple marinade for beef uses lime juice, soy sauce, finely chopped onion and garlic, as well as olive oil and pureed adobo chili. This will give the meat a deep, rich flavor while also improving texture. This is particularly good for tougher, cheaper cuts like flap meat or flank steak. And marinades aren't just for meat. You can also use marinades to add flavor to vegetables. Sliced zucchini marinated in olive oil, salt, and a pinch of cayenne pepper is packed with flavor and a little heat. You can also use balsamic vinegar in place of the cayenne pepper to add a little sweetness.

DRY AGE AND GRILL YOUR BEEF FOR PROFESSIONAL RESULTS

While buying meat, you may have noticed that the more expensive beef has been dry aged. We're going to discuss why dry aging is important, how it works, and how you can do it yourself at home. Dry aging is a process designed to get the most flavor out of your beef. This is done by concentrating the flavor by removing excess water. Now, you might be thinking… If you get rid of water in the meat, won't the meat be dry? The simple answer is, no. Meat does not get its juiciness from water. The juiciness comes from rendering fat and the fat is not affected by dry aging. In reality, the more water that your meat is retaining, the more the flavor is diluted. To add more flavor, remove the water. Butcher shops do this by aging entire sides of meat at the same time by allowing the meat to sit, salted and uncovered, in the refrigerator for a period of twenty and forty days. The salt will add flavor to the meat and it will also keep any harmful bacteria away. The salt will also help to naturally draw the excess water out of the meat. Because the meat is uncovered, it will naturally evaporate in the refrigerator.

To do this at home, all you need to do is buy some steaks. For best grilling results, we suggest steaks that have been cut to around one and a half to two inches thick. Sprinkle the exterior of the steaks with a generous amount of salt so it is uniformly coated. Then place the steaks in a wire rack over a rimmed baking sheet. You want the entire surface of the steak to be exposed to the air. Place the steaks in the fridge and simply wait. For meat that has already been cut into steaks there is no reason to dry age for more than a few days. Once your steaks have aged in the refrigerator for a few days and you're ready to cook, remove them from the refrigerator and pat dry with paper towels. In order to get the best sear on any kind of meat it is important to make sure the surface is completely dry. Otherwise, the moisture on the surface will produce steam when it touches the heat.

Right before you cook, you may add some black pepper for a little extra flavor. For steaks like New York Strip and Rib-eye, set your gas grill to it's highest possible heat. Wait for the grates to get as hot as possible and then add the steaks. Allow the steaks to cook without flipping for several minutes. If they stick to the grill, that just means they're not ready to flip yet, so leave them alone. Most chefs agree that medium-rare is the perfect temperature for steaks and you can make sure you get a perfect medium-rare by using an instant read thermometer to test the middle of your steak. When it reaches 125F remove it from the grill and place it on a cutting board to rest. Make sure to give steak ten to twelve minutes to rest before cutting. If you don't rest the steak long enough, the juices will not have time to reabsorb into the meat and they will bleed out, leaving you with dry, tough meat. Once your steaks are rested, either slice or serve whole.

CHAPTER 4
MAIN DISHES: POULTRY

SWEET ORANGE CHILI LIME CHICKEN

SERVINGS: 4

Prep time: 35 minutes
Cook time: 15 minutes

INGREDIENTS

1/2 cup sweet chili sauce

1/4 cup soy sauce

1 teaspoon mirin

1 teaspoon orange juice, fresh squeezed

1 teaspoon orange marmalade

2 tablespoons lime juice

1 tablespoon brown sugar

1 clove garlic, minced

4 boneless, skinless chicken breasts

Sesame seeds, for garnish

Sweet and citrus marinated chicken is the perfect way to get some good use out of your gas grill. Pair this citrus sweet medley with grilled vegetables and brown rice for a quick weeknight meal.

DIRECTIONS

1. Whisk sweet chili sauce, soy sauce, mirin, orange marmalade, lime and orange juice, brown sugar, and minced garlic together in a small mixing bowl.
2. Set aside 1/4 cup of the sauce.
3. Toss chicken in sauce to coat and marinate 30 minutes.
4. Preheat your grill to medium heat.
5. Put the chicken on the grill and grill each side for 7 minutes.
6. Baste the cooked chicken with remaining marinade and garnish with sesame seeds to serve with your favorite sides.

Nutritional Info: Calories: 380, Sodium: 1274mg, Dietary Fiber: 0.5g, Fat: 12g, Carbs: 19.7g, Protein: 43.8g.

ZESTY CHILI LIME CHICKEN

SERVINGS: 4

Prep time: 8 - 24 hours
Cook time: 20 minutes

INGREDIENTS

2 lbs. Boneless, skinless chicken thighs

FOR THE MARINADE:

1/4 cup fresh lime juice
2 teaspoons lime zest
1/4 cup honey
2 tablespoons olive oil
1 tablespoon balsamic vinegar
1/2 teaspoon sea salt
1/2 teaspoon black pepper
2 garlic cloves, minced
1/4 teaspoon onion powder

Whip up something super-quick and easy for family dinner night. This is one delicious chicken recipe the whole family will love. Serve this delicious chicken with a side of grilled romaine or your favorite vegetables.

DIRECTIONS

1. Whisk together marinade ingredients in a large mixing bowl; reserve 2 tablespoons of the marinade for grilling.
2. Add chicken and marinade to a sealable plastic bag and marinate 8 hours or overnight in the refrigerator.
3. Preheat grill to medium high heat and brush lightly with olive oil.
4. Place chicken on grill and cook 8 minutes per side.
5. Baste each side of chicken with reserved marinade during the last few minutes of cooking; chicken is done when the internal temperature reaches 165 degrees Fahrenheit.
6. Plate chicken, tent with foil, and allow to rest for 5 minutes.
7. Serve and enjoy!

Nutritional Info: Calories: 381, Sodium: 337mg, Dietary Fiber: 1.1g, Fat: 20.2g, Carbs: 4.7g, Protein: 44.7g.

CLASSIC BBQ CHICKEN

SERVINGS: 4 - 6

Prep time: 5 minutes
Cook time: 1 hour 45 minutes

INGREDIENTS

4 pounds of your favorite chicken, including legs, thighs, wings, and breasts, skin-on

Salt

Olive oil

1 cup barbecue sauce, like Hickory Mesquite or Homemade

BBQ Chicken has never tasted so good! We love this classic BBQ favorite for a taste of summer all year around. Simply serve with your favorite side dishes for a full family style meal.

DIRECTIONS

1. Rub the chicken with olive oil and salt.
2. Preheat the grill to high heat.
3. Sear chicken skin side down on the grill for 5-10 minutes.
4. Turn the grill down to medium low heat, tent with foil and cook for 30 minutes.
5. Turn chicken and baste with barbecue sauce.
6. Cover the chicken again and allow to cook for another 20 minutes.
7. Baste, cover and cook again for 30 minutes; repeat basting and turning during this time.
8. The chicken is done when the internal temperature of the chicken pieces are 165°F and juices run clear.
9. Baste with more barbecue sauce to serve!

Nutritional Info: Calories: 539, Sodium: 684mg, Dietary Fiber: 0.3g, Fat: 11.6g, Carbs: 15.1g, Protein: 87.6g.

CHIPOTLE ADOBE CHICKEN

SERVINGS: 4 - 6

Prep Time: 1 - 24 hours
Cook Time: 20 minutes

Smoky sweet chipotle peppers in adobo sauce make for one delicious marinade! Perfect served with yellow Mexican rice or cheese enchiladas for one hearty Mexican inspired meal.

INGREDIENTS

2 lbs chicken thighs or breasts (boneless, skinless)

FOR THE MARINADE:

1/4 cup olive oil

2 chipotle peppers in adobo sauce, plus 1 teaspoon adobo sauce from the can

1 tablespoon garlic, minced

1 shallot, finely chopped

1-1/2 tablespoons cumin

1 tablespoon cilantro, super-finely chopped or dried

2 teaspoons chili powder

1 teaspoon dried oregano

1/2 teaspoon salt

Fresh limes, for garnish

Cilantro, for garnish

DIRECTIONS

1. Preheat grill to medium-high.
2. Add marinade ingredients to a food processor or blender and pulse into a paste.
3. Add the chicken and marinade to a sealable plastic bag, and coat well.
4. Place in the refrigerator for 1 hour to 24 hours before grilling.
5. Grill chicken for 7 minutes, turn and grill an additional 7 minutes; or until good grill marks appear.
6. Turn heat to low and continue to grill until chicken is cooked through and internal temperature reaches 165 degrees Fahrenheit.
7. Remove chicken from grill and allow to rest 5 to 10 minutes before serving.
8. Garnish with a squeeze of fresh lime and a sprinkle of cilantro to serve.

Nutritional Info: Calories: 561, Sodium: 431mg, Dietary Fiber: 0.3g, Fat: 23.8g, Carbs: 18.7g, Protein: 65.9g.

HONEY BALSAMIC MARINATED CHICKEN

SERVINGS: 4

Prep time: 30 minutes - 4 hours
Cook time: 20 minutes

INGREDIENTS

2 lbs. boneless, skinless chicken thighs

1 teaspoon olive oil

1/2 teaspoon sea salt

1/4 teaspoon black pepper

1/2 teaspoon paprika

3/4 teaspoon onion powder

FOR THE MARINADE:

2 tablespoons honey

2 tablespoons balsamic vinegar

2 tablespoons tomato paste

1 teaspoon garlic, minced

Sweet honey meets balsamic vinegar for a delicious marinated chicken that is perfect for your gas grill. Perfect served with your favorite sides or on a fluffy bed of brown rice.

DIRECTIONS

1. Add chicken, olive oil, salt, black pepper, paprika, and onion powder to a sealable plastic bag. Seal and toss to coat, covering chicken with spices and oil; set aside.
2. Whisk together balsamic vinegar, tomato paste, garlic, and honey.
3. Divide the marinade in half. Add one half to the bag of chicken and store the other half in a sealed container in the refrigerator.
4. Seal the bag and toss chicken to coat. Refrigerate for 30 minutes to 4 hours.
5. Preheat a grill to medium-high.
6. Discard bag and marinade. Add chicken to the grill and cook 7 minutes per side or until juices run clear and a meat thermometer reads 165 degrees Fahrenheit.
7. During last minute of cooking, brush remaining marinade on top of the chicken thighs.
8. Serve immediately.

Nutritional Info: Calories: 485, Sodium: 438mg, Dietary Fiber: 0.5g, Fat: 18.1g, Carbs: 11g, Protein: 66.1g.

CALIFORNIA GRILLED CHICKEN

SERVINGS: 4

Prep time: 35 minutes
Cook time: 20 minutes

Classic, ripe, and fresh California ingredients transform ordinary chicken into one scrumptious meal.

INGREDIENTS

4 boneless, skinless chicken breasts

3/4 cup balsamic vinegar

2 tablespoons extra virgin olive oil

1 tablespoon honey

1 teaspoon oregano

1 teaspoon basil

1 teaspoon garlic powder

FOR GARNISH:

Sea salt

Black pepper, fresh ground

4 slices fresh mozzarella cheese

4 slices avocado

4 slices beefsteak tomato

Balsamic glaze, for drizzling

DIRECTIONS

1. Whisk together balsamic vinegar, honey, olive oil, oregano, basil and garlic powder in a large mixing bowl.
2. Add chicken to coat and marinate for 30 minutes in the refrigerator.
3. Preheat grill to medium-high. Grill chicken for 7 minutes per side, or until a meat thermometer reaches 165°F.
4. Top each chicken breast with mozzarella, avocado, and tomato and tent with foil on the grill to melt for 2 minutes.
5. Garnish with a drizzle of balsamic glaze, and a pinch of sea salt and black pepper.

Nutritional Info: Calories: 883, Sodium: 449mg, Dietary Fiber: 15.2g, Fat: 62.1g, Carbs: 29.8g, Protein: 55.3g.

SALSA VERDE MARINATED CHICKEN

SERVINGS: 6

Prep time: 4 hours 35 minutes
Cook time: 4 hours 50 minutes

INGREDIENTS

6 boneless, skinless chicken breasts

1 tablespoon olive oil

1 teaspoon sea salt

1 teaspoon chili powder

1 teaspoon ground cumin

1 teaspoon garlic powder

FOR THE SALSA VERDE MARINADE:

3 teaspoons garlic, minced

1 small onion, chopped

6 tomatillos, husked, rinsed and chopped

1 medium jalapeño pepper, cut in half, seeded

1/4 cup fresh cilantro, chopped

1/2 teaspoon sugar or sugar substitute

Spicy salsa verde is the perfect compliment to savory grilled chicken. When you want to spice things up on the grill, this is just the recipe to help you add some spice to your life!

DIRECTIONS

1. Add salsa verde marinade ingredients to a food processor and pulse until smooth.
2. Mix sea salt, chili powder, cumin, and garlic powder together in a small mixing bowl.
3. Season chicken breasts with olive oil and seasoning mix, and lay in glass baking dish.
4. Spread a tablespoon of salsa verde marinade over each chicken breast to cover; reserve remaining salsa for serving.
5. Cover dish with plastic wrap and refrigerate for 4 hours.
6. Preheat grill to medium-high and brush with olive oil.
7. Add chicken to grill and cook 7 minutes per side or until juices run clear and a meat thermometer reads 165°F.
8. Serve each with additional salsa verde and enjoy!

Nutritional Info: Calories: 321, Sodium: 444mg, Dietary Fiber: 1.3g, Fat: 13.7g, Carbs: 4.8g, Protein: 43g.

CHICKEN WINGS WITH SWEET RED CHILI AND PEACH GLAZE

SERVINGS: 4

Prep time: 15 minutes
Cook time: 30 minutes

INGREDIENTS

1 (12 oz.) jar peach preserves
1 cup sweet red chili sauce
1 teaspoon lime juice
1 tablespoon fresh cilantro, minced
1 (2-1/2 lb.) bag chicken wing sections
Non-stick cooking spray

Whip up delicious, restaurant style chicken wings right at home with your gas grill. Sweet and savory, these chicken wings are the perfect treat for any game day or Sunday Funday with the family.

DIRECTIONS

1. Mix preserves, red chili sauce, lime juice and cilantro in mixing bowl. Divide in half, and place one half aside for serving.
2. Preheat grill to medium heat and spray with non-stick cooking spray.
3. Grill wings for 25 minutes turning several times until juices run clear.
4. Remove wings from grill, toss in a bowl to coat wings with remaining glaze.
5. Return wings to grill and cook for an additional 3 to 5 minutes turning once.
6. Serve warm with your favorite dips and side dishes!

Nutritional Info: Calories: 790, Sodium: 643mg, Dietary Fiber: 1g, Fat: 16.9g, Carbs: 87.5g, Protein: 66g.

HAWAIIAN CHICKEN SKEWERS

SERVINGS: 4 - 5

Prep Time: 1 hour 10 minutes
Cook Time: 15 minutes

INGREDIENTS

1 lb. boneless, skinless chicken breast, cut into 1-1/2 inch cubes

3 cups pineapple, cut into 1-1/2 inch cubes

2 large green peppers, cut into 1-1/2 inch pieces

1 large red onion, cut into 1 1/2 inch pieces

2 tablespoons olive oil, to coat veggies

FOR THE MARINADE:

1/3 cup tomato paste

1/3 cup brown sugar, packed

1/3 cup soy sauce

1/4 cup pineapple juice

2 tablespoons olive oil

1-1/2 tablespoon mirin or rice wine vinegar

4 teaspoons garlic cloves, minced

1 tablespoon ginger, minced

1/2 teaspoon sesame oil

Pinch of sea salt

Pinch of ground black pepper

10 wooden skewers, for assembly

Grill up a taste of Hawaii with these delicious chicken skewers! Super-easy to make, you can enjoy these yummy skewers any night of the week - just prep them a day before grilling for one easy dinner in no time.

DIRECTIONS

1. Combine marinade ingredients in a mixing bowl until smooth. Reserve a 1/2 cup of the marinade in the refrigerator.
2. Add chicken and remaining marinade to a sealable plastic bag and refrigerate for 1 hour.
3. Soak 10 wooden skewer sticks in water for 1 hour.
4. Preheat the grill to medium heat.
5. Add red onion, bell pepper and pineapple to a mixing bowl with 2 tablespoons olive oil and toss to coat.
6. Thread red onion, bell pepper, pineapple and chicken onto the skewers until all of the chicken has been used.
7. Place skewers on grill and grab your reserved marinade from the refrigerator; grill for 5 minutes then brush with remaining marinade and rotate.
8. Brush again with marinade and grill about 5 additional minutes or until chicken reads 165°F on a meat thermometer.
9. Serve warm.

Nutritional Info: Calories: 311, Sodium: 1116mg, Dietary Fiber: 4.2g, Fat: 8.8g, Carbs: 38.1g, Protein: 22.8g.

CHICKEN TACOS WITH AVOCADO CREMA

SERVINGS: 4 - 5

Prep Time: 1 hour 5 minutes
Cook Time: 10 minutes

INGREDIENTS

1-1/2 lbs. Boneless, skinless chicken breasts, sliced thin

FOR THE CHICKEN MARINADE:

1 serrano pepper, minced

2 teaspoons garlic, minced

1 lime, juiced

1 teaspoon ground cumin

1/3 cup olive oil

Sea salt, to taste

Black pepper, to taste

FOR THE AVOCADO CREMA:

1 cup sour cream

2 teaspoons lime juice

1 teaspoon lime zest

1 serrano pepper, diced and seeded

1 clove garlic, minced

1 large hass avocado

FOR THE GARNISH:

1/2 cup queso fresco, crumbled

2 teaspoons cilantro, chopped

1 lime sliced into wedges

10 corn tortillas

The perfect way to do lunch prep on a Sunday, you can whip this recipe up in no time and eat it for lunch during the week. The whole family will enjoy these delicious tacos! Just keep your avocado crema in a sealable container.

DIRECTIONS

1. Mix chicken marinade together in a sealable plastic bag. Add chicken and toss to coat well.

2. Marinate for 1 hour in the refrigerator.

3. Combine avocado crema ingredients in a food processor or blender and pulse until smooth.

4. Cover and refrigerate until you are ready to assemble tacos.

5. Preheat grill to medium heat and grill chicken for 5 minutes per side; rotating and turning as needed.

6. Remove from grill and tent loosely with aluminum foil. Allow chicken to rest 5 minutes.

7. Serve with warm tortillas, a dollop of avocado crema, queso fresco, cilantro and lime wedges.

8. To meal prep: simply divide chicken into individual portion containers with a serving of the garnish, and take with tortillas wrapped in parchment paper to warm in a microwave to serve.

Nutritional Info: Calories: 703, Sodium: 357mg, Dietary Fiber: 6.3g, Fat: 44.5g, Carbs:30.5g, Protein: 47.9g.

KALE CAESAR SALAD WITH GRILLED CHICKEN

SERVINGS: 1

Prep time: 10 minutes
Cook time: 8 minutes

Light and airy, Caesar Salad is delicious tossed with grilled chicken and kale. You'll love this easy recipe that cooks up in no time - so you can enjoy healthy meals every day of the week!

INGREDIENTS

1 chicken breast
1 teaspoon garlic powder
1/2 teaspoon black pepper
1/2 teaspoon sea salt
2 kale leaves, chopped
Shaved parmesan, for serving

FOR THE DRESSING:

1 tablespoon mayonnaise
1/2 tablespoon Dijon mustard
1/2 teaspoon garlic powder
1/2 teaspoon Worcestershire sauce
1/4 lemon, juice of (or 1/2 of a small lime)
1/4 teaspoon anchovy paste
Pinch of sea salt
Pinch of black pepper

DIRECTIONS

1. Mix garlic powder, black pepper, and sea salt in a small mixing bowl. Coat chicken with seasoning mix.
2. Preheat grill to medium-high heat.
3. Grill chicken on each side for 7 minutes or until a meat thermometer reads 165°F when inserted in the thickest part of the breast.
4. Whisk all of the dressing ingredients together.
5. Plate your kale and pour the dressing over, and toss to combine.
6. Cut the grilled chicken on a diagonal and place on top of the salad. Garnish with shaved parmesan, and serve.

Nutritional Info: Calories: 643, Sodium: 1549mg, Dietary Fiber: 3.8g, Fat: 18.6g, Carbs: 26.3g, Protein: 93.3g.

HASSELBACK STUFFED CHICKEN

SERVINGS: 4

Prep time: 15 minutes
Cook time: 30 minutes

INGREDIENTS

4 boneless, skinless chicken breasts

2 tablespoons olive oil

2 tablespoons taco seasoning

1/2 red, yellow and green pepper, very thinly sliced

1 small red onion, very thinly sliced

1/2 cup Mexican shredded cheese

Guacamole, for serving

Sour cream, for serving

Salsa, for serving

Who doesn't love chicken breast seasoned to perfection and grilled like hasselback potatoes?! This delicious recipe is gluten-free and diabetic friendly for one delicious dinner that you can serve with salad or steamed veggies.

DIRECTIONS

1. Preheat grill to med-high.
2. Cut thin horizontal cuts across each chicken breast; like you would hasselback potatoes.
3. Rub chicken evenly with olive oil and taco seasoning.
4. Add a mixture of bell peppers and red onions to each cut, and place the breasts on the grill.
5. Cook chicken for 15 minutes.
6. Remove and top with cheese.
7. Tent loosely with foil and Grill another 5 minutes, until cheese is melted.
8. Remove from grill and top with guacamole, sour cream and salsa. Serve alongside your favorite side dishes!

Nutritional Info: Calories: 643, Sodium: 1549mg, Dietary Fiber: 3.8g, Fat: 18.6g, Carbs: 26.3g, Protein: 93.3g.

FIERY ITALIAN CHICKEN SKEWERS

SERVINGS: 2 - 4

Prep time: 1 hour 20 minutes
Cook time: 20 minutes

INGREDIENTS

10 boneless, skinless chicken thighs, cut into chunks

1 large red onion, cut into wedges

1 large red pepper, stemmed, seeded, and cut into chunks

FOR THE MARINADE:

1/3 cup toasted pine nuts

1-1/2 cups sliced roasted red peppers

5 hot cherry peppers, stemmed and seeded, or to taste

1 cup packed fresh basil leaves, plus more to serve

4 cloves garlic, peeled

1/4 cup grated Parmesan cheese

1 tablespoon paprika

Extra virgin olive oil, as needed

Fire up some yummy chicken skewers on your gas grill and really shake things up for lunch or dinner. You'll love how easy it is to make these perfectly seasoned skewers any day of the week.

DIRECTIONS

1. Combine the toasted pine nuts, roasted red peppers, hot cherry peppers, basil, garlic, Parmesan, and paprika in a food processor or blender and process until well-combined.
2. Add in olive oil until the pesto reaches a thin consistency in order to coat the chicken as a marinade.
3. Transfer half of the pesto to a large sealable plastic bag, and reserve the other half for serving.
4. Add the chicken thigh chunks to the bag of pesto, seal, and massage the bag to coat the chicken.
5. Refrigerate for 1 hour.
6. Preheat grill to medium-high heat and brush with olive oil.
7. Thread the chicken cubes, red onion, and red pepper onto metal skewers.
8. Brush the chicken with the reserved pesto.
9. Grill until the chicken reaches an internal temperature of 165°F; about 5 minutes per side. Serve warm with your favorite salad or vegetables!

Nutritional Info: Calories: 945, Sodium: 798mg, Dietary Fiber: 3.2g, Fat: 46.7g, Carbs: 14.7g, Protein: 112.2g.

CREOLE CHICKEN STUFFED WITH CHEESE & PEPPERS

SERVINGS: 4

Prep time: 10 minutes
Cook time: 20 minutes

INGREDIENTS

4 boneless, skinless chicken breasts

8 mini sweet peppers, sliced thin and seeded

2 slices pepper jack cheese, cut in half

2 slices Colby jack cheese, cut in half

1 tablespoon creole seasoning, like Emeril's

1 teaspoon black pepper

1 teaspoon garlic powder

1 teaspoon onion powder

4 teaspoons olive oil, separated

Toothpicks

Nothing beats a grilled stuffed chicken breast that preps in 10 minutes. This easy to assemble recipe will have your family eating healthy even on busy weeknights!

DIRECTIONS

1. Rinse chicken and pat dry.
2. Mix creole seasoning, pepper, garlic powder, and onion powder together in a small mixing bowl and set aside.
3. Cut a slit on the side of each chicken breast; be careful not to cut all the way through the chicken.
4. Rub each breast with 1 teaspoon each of olive oil.
5. Rub each chicken breast with seasoning mix and coat evenly.
6. Stuff each breast of chicken with 1 half pepper jack cheese slice, 1 half colby cheese slice, and a handful of pepper slices.
7. Secure chicken shut with 4 or 5 toothpicks.
8. Preheat the grill to medium-high and cook chicken for 8 minutes per side; or until chicken reaches an internal temperature of 165 degrees Fahrenheit.
9. Allow chicken to rest for 5 minutes, remove toothpicks, and serve.

Nutritional Info: Calories: 509, Sodium: 1117mg, Dietary Fiber: 3.4g, Fat: 25.1g, Carbs: 19.8g, Protein: 51.4g.

TERIYAKI CHICKEN AND VEGGIE RICE BOWLS

SERVINGS: 4

Prep time: 8 hours 10 minutes
Cook time: 20 minutes

Rice bowls are both delicious and nutritious and a perfect way to meal prep on a Sunday for the whole week. This recipe will keep in your refrigerator for up to 4 days once cooked and makes for a delicious meal at work or school when microwaved!

INGREDIENTS

1 bag brown rice

FOR THE SKEWERS:

2 boneless skinless chicken breasts, cubed
1 red onion, quartered
1 red pepper, cut into cube slices
1 green pepper, cut into cube slices
1/2 pineapple, cut into cubes

FOR THE MARINADE:

1/4 cup light soy sauce
1/4 cup sesame oil
1 tablespoon ginger, fresh grated
1 garlic clove, crushed
1/2 lime, juiced

DIRECTIONS

1. Whisk the marinade ingredients together in a small mixing bowl.
2. Add chicken and marinade to a resealable plastic bag, seal and toss well to coat.
3. Refrigerate for one hour or over night.
4. Prepare rice as instructed on the bag.
5. Preheat the grill to medium-high heat.
6. Thread the chicken and the cubed veggies onto 8 metal skewers and grill for 8 minutes on each side until charred and cooked through.
7. Portion rice out into bowls and top with two skewers each, and enjoy!

Nutritional Info: Calories: 477, Sodium: 362mg, Dietary Fiber: 3.8g, Fat: 20.6g, Carbs: 48.1g, Protein: 26.1g.

YELLOW CURRY CHICKEN WINGS

SERVINGS: 6

Prep time: 35 minutes
Cook time: 30 minutes to 1 hour

INGREDIENTS

2 lbs. chicken wings

FOR THE MARINADE:

1/2 cup Greek yogurt, plain

1 tablespoon mild yellow curry powder

1 tablespoon olive oil

1/2 teaspoon sea salt

1/2 teaspoon black pepper

1 teaspoon red chili flakes

Warm and savory, these grilled chicken wings are sure to spice things up with a taste of India. Curry Grilled Chicken Wings are best served with poppadoms, chutney, and raita dip for a delicious party snack.

DIRECTIONS

1. Rinse and pat wings dry with paper towels.
2. Whisk marinade ingredients together in a large mixing bowl until well-combined.
3. Add wings to bowl and toss to coat.
4. Cover bowl with plastic wrap and chill in the refrigerator for 30 minutes.
5. Prepare one side of the grill for medium heat and the other side on medium-high.
6. Working in batches, grill wings over medium heat, turning occasionally, until skin starts to brown; about 12 minutes.
7. Move wings to medium-high area of grill for 5 minutes on each side to char until cooked through; meat thermometer should register 165°F when touching the bone.
8. Transfer wings to a platter and serve warm.

Nutritional Info: Calories: 324, Sodium: 292mg, Dietary Fiber: 0.4g, Fat: 14g, Carbs: 1.4g, Protein: 45.6g.

KOREAN GRILLED CHICKEN WINGS WITH SCALLION

SERVINGS: 6

Prep time: 30 minutes
Cook time: 30 minutes to 1 hour

INGREDIENTS

2 pounds chicken wings (flats and drumettes attached or separated)

FOR THE MARINADE:

1 tablespoon olive oil

1 teaspoon sea salt, plus more

1/2 teaspoon black pepper

1/2 cup gochujang, Korean hot pepper paste

1 scallion, thinly sliced, for garnish

Grilled chicken wings are perfect when seasoned with the spice of Gochujang. This recipe pairs perfect with a Japanese White Sauce or cool, creamy sour cream infused with lime zest. Serve them up for your next tailgate or dinner party for something elevated and fun.

DIRECTIONS

1. Rinse and pat wings dry with paper towels.
2. Whisk marinade ingredients together in a large mixing bowl until well-combined.
3. Add wings to bowl and toss to coat.
4. Cover bowl with plastic wrap and chill in the refrigerator for 30 minutes.
5. Prepare one side of the grill for medium heat and the other side on medium-high.
6. Working in batches, grill wings over medium heat, turning occasionally, until skin starts to brown; about 12 minutes.
7. Move wings to medium-high area of grill for 5 minutes on each side to char until cooked through; meat thermometer should register 165°F when touching the bone.
8. Transfer wings to a platter, garnish with scallions, and serve warm with your favorite dipping sauces.

Nutritional Info: Calories: 312, Sodium: 476mg, Dietary Fiber: 0.4g, Fat: 13.5g, Carbs: 1.1g, Protein: 43.9g.

BUFFALO GRILLED CHICKEN WINGS

SERVINGS: 6 - 8

Prep time: 10 minutes
Cook time: 20 minutes

INGREDIENTS

1 tablespoon sea salt

1 teaspoon ground black pepper

1 teaspoon garlic powder

3 lbs. chicken wings

6 tablespoons unsalted butter

1/3 cup buffalo sauce, like Moore's

1 tablespoon apple cider vinegar

1 tablespoon honey

Craving restaurant style Buffalo Wings?! You can easily whip them up right at home with this quick and easy recipe. Serve them with your favorite dips, carrots and celery for a fun treat.

DIRECTIONS

1. Combine salt, pepper and garlic powder in a large mixing bowl.
2. Toss the wings with the seasoning mixture to coat.
3. Preheat grill to medium heat.
4. Place the wings on the grill; make sure they are touching so the meat stays moist on the bone while grilling.
5. Flip wings every 5 minutes, for a total of 20 minutes of cooking.
6. Heat the butter, buffalo sauce, vinegar and honey in a saucepan over low heat; whisk to combine well.
7. Add wings to a large mixing bowl, toss the wings with the sauce to coat.
8. Turn grill up to medium high and place wings back on the grill until the skins crisp; about 1 to 2 minutes per side.
9. Add wings back into the bowl with the sauce and toss to serve.

Nutritional Info: Calories: 410, Sodium: 950mg, Dietary Fiber: 0.2g, Fat: 21.3g, Carbs: 2.7g, Protein: 49.4g.

POPPYSEED CHICKEN SUMMER SALAD

SERVINGS: 3

Prep time: 5 minutes
Cook time: 25 minutes

INGREDIENTS

3 boneless chicken breast halves

1/4 cup poppy seed dressing, plus 1/2 cup for basting chicken

1 bag (8 oz.) romaine salad

1 cup fresh blueberries, rinsed

1 cup strawberries, sliced

1/4 cup almonds, sliced

Sea salt, for seasoning

Black pepper, for seasoning

Grilled Chicken Summer Salads are a refreshing and delicious way to enjoy your gas grill! Pair it with a cool, crisp glass of lemonade or sparkling water - and you've got one delicious meal.

DIRECTIONS

1. Baste chicken with 1/2 cup poppyseed dressing. Season each chicken breast with a pinch of pepper and sea salt.
2. Preheat grill to medium heat.
3. Grill chicken for 10 minutes on each side or until chicken is no longer pink in center; brushing occasionally with more poppyseed dressing.
4. Let chicken rest for five minutes.
5. Toss lettuce mix with remaining 1/4 cup of dressing.
6. Portion salad evenly into three bowls and top each with an even amount of blueberries and strawberries.
7. Cut chicken crosswise into 1/2 inch thick slices.
8. Arrange one sliced chicken breast on each salad bowl and sprinkle almonds to serve.

Nutritional Info: Calories: 479, Sodium: 405mg, Dietary Fiber: 3.1g, Fat: 25.8g, Carbs: 16.2g, Protein: 45.2g.

LEMON GINGER CHICKEN WITH FRUIT SALSA

SERVINGS: 4

Prep time: 1 hour
Cook time: 20 minutes

INGREDIENTS

4 boneless, skinless chicken breasts

FOR THE MARINADE:

1/2 cup fresh lemon juice

1/2 cup soy sauce

1 tablespoon fresh ginger, minced

1 tablespoon lemon pepper seasoning

2 garlic cloves, minced

FOR THE SALSA:

1-1/2 cups pineapple, chopped

3/4 cup kiwi fruit, chopped

1/2 cup mango, chopped

1/2 cup red onion, finely chopped

2 tablespoons fresh cilantro, chopped

1 small jalapeño pepper, seeded and chopped

1-1/2 teaspoons ground cumin

1/4 teaspoon sea salt

1/8 teaspoon black pepper

1/2 teaspoon olive oil, more for brushing grill

Fruit salsa is the perfect compliment to any grilled chicken. This zesty recipe is sure to knock the socks off the ones you love for a delicious healthy weekend meal on the grill! Simply serve with grilled veggies on the side for a healthy treat.

DIRECTIONS

1. Combine marinade ingredients in a large sealable plastic bag.
2. Add chicken to bag, seal, and toss to coat. Marinate in refrigerator for 1 hour.
3. Combine salsa ingredients in a mixing bowl and toss gently to combine. Set aside until ready to serve.
4. Preheat the grill.
5. Remove chicken from bag and discard marinade.
6. Brush grill with olive oil and cook chicken for 7 minutes on each side or until chicken is cooked through.
7. Serve chicken topped with salsa alongside your favorite side dishes.

Nutritional Info: Calories: 391, Sodium: 2051mg, Dietary Fiber: 3.7g, Fat: 12.3g, Carbs: 23.6g, Protein: 46.1g.

LEMON-OLIVE GRILLED CHICKEN

SERVINGS: 4

Prep time: 30 minutes
Cook time: 20 minutes

INGREDIENTS

1 lbs. chicken breast tenders

1 shallot, chopped

FOR THE MARINADE:

1 lemon, juiced

1 teaspoon lemon zest

4 teaspoons olive oil

1/2 teaspoon sea salt

1/2 teaspoon white pepper

1 teaspoon sugar

1/4 cup white wine, like Chardonnay

The bright zest of lemon brightens this grilled chicken with a delightful summer taste. Best served with salad and risotto, you can prepare this chicken in no time!

DIRECTIONS

1. Mix marinade ingredients together in a mixing bowl; when well combined incorporate chopped shallot and chicken to coat well.
2. Cover and marinate for 30 minutes in the refrigerator.
3. Preheat grill to medium-high. Grill chicken for 7 minutes per side, or until a meat thermometer reaches 165°F.
4. Allow chicken to rest for 5 minutes after grilling and serve with your favorite sides.

Nutritional Info: Calories: 166, Sodium: 458mg, Dietary Fiber: 0.7g, Fat: 5.3g, Carbs: 4g, Protein: 22.6g.

CHICKEN THIGHS WITH GINGER-SESAME GLAZE

SERVINGS: 4 - 8

Prep time: 10 minutes
Cook time: 20 minutes

INGREDIENTS

8 boneless, skinless chicken thighs

FOR THE GLAZE:

3 tablespoons dark brown sugar

2-1/2 tablespoons soy sauce

1 tablespoon fresh garlic, minced

2 teaspoons sesame seeds

1 teaspoon fresh ginger, minced

1 teaspoon sambal oelek

1/3 cup scallions, thinly sliced

Non-stick cooking spray

Ginger and sesame come together in this delicious glaze for a taste explosion. Serve this warm and sweet chicken with brown rice and your favorite vegetables for a quick, Asian-inspired meal.

DIRECTIONS

1. Combine glaze ingredients in a large mixing bowl; separate and reserve half for serving.
2. Add chicken to bowl and toss to coat well.
3. Preheat the grill to medium-high heat.
4. Coat with cooking spray.
5. Cook chicken for 6 minutes on each side or until done.
6. Transfer chicken to plates and drizzle with remaining glaze to serve.

Nutritional Info: Calories: 301, Sodium: 413mg, Dietary Fiber: 0.3g, Fat: 11.2g, Carbs: 4.7g, Protein: 42.9g.

SOBA NOODLE CHICKEN WITH MISO VINAIGRETTE

SERVINGS: 2

Prep time: 10 minutes
Cook time: 20 minutes

Watching your carbs or gluten intake? This is the perfect meal for a romantic evening. Just be sure to pick soba noodles labeled gluten-free..

INGREDIENTS

1 package gluten-free soba noodles

1 teaspoon black sesame seeds, for garnish

2 skinless, boneless chicken breasts, halved like cutlets

1/2 teaspoon freshly ground black pepper

1/4 teaspoon kosher salt

FOR THE MARINADE:

2 tablespoons olive oil

1 tablespoon white miso, or soybean paste

1 tablespoon mirin

1 tablespoon soy sauce

2 teaspoons sesame oil

1-1/2 teaspoons fresh ginger, minced

1 teaspoon honey

FOR THE VEGGIES:

1/2 cup carrot, shredded

1-1/2 cups red cabbage, thin sliced

1/2 cup green onions, sliced

Olive oil, for brushing

DIRECTIONS

1. Prepare soba noodles according to package instructions.
2. Drain; rinse with cold water and drain again. Set aside.
3. Preheat one side of the grill to medium heat and one side to medium high heat.
4. Combine marinade ingredients in a large mixing bowl.
5. Add 2 tablespoons of the marinade to a second mixing bowl and set aside.
6. Sprinkle chicken with pepper and salt, and add chicken to marinade bowl.
7. Brush grill with olive oil.
8. Add veggies to the medium heat side and sauté for 5 minutes.
9. Add chicken to the medium high side and cook 7 minutes on each side or until done.
10. Add noodles and veggies to the reserved bowl of marinade. Toss to coat well and return to grill for 3 minutes.
11. Remove food from grill to plate, sprinkle noodles with sesame seeds, and serve warm.

Nutritional Info: Calories: 625, Sodium: 1512mg, Dietary Fiber: 3.7g, Fat: 31g, Carbs: 39.8g, Protein: 49.7g.

CHICKEN SATAY WITH ALMOND BUTTER SAUCE

SERVINGS: 4

Prep time: 2 hours 20 minutes
Cook time: 8 minutes

INGREDIENTS

1 lb. boneless, skinless chicken thighs, cut into thin strips

Olive oil, for brushing

FOR THE MARINADE:

1/2 cup canned light coconut milk

1/2 lime, juiced

1 tablespoon honey

2 teaspoons soy sauce

1-1/2 teaspoons fish sauce

1/2 teaspoon red chili flakes

2 teaspoons ginger, grated

1 clove of garlic, grated

1/2 teaspoon curry powder

1/4 teaspoon ground coriander

FOR THE ALMOND BUTTER SAUCE:

1/4 cup almond butter

1/4 cup water

2 tablespoons canned, light coconut milk

1 tablespoon honey

1/2 lime, juiced

1 teaspoon fish sauce

1 teaspoon fresh grated ginger

1/2 teaspoon low sodium soy sauce

1/2 teaspoon Sriracha

A mouthwatering, sweet meets spicy delight - this recipe is delicious served as an appetizer for dipping or over a bed of pad Thai noodles for an Asian-inspired dish. Serve it garnished with lime wedges and crushed peanuts for something out of this world.

DIRECTIONS

1. Whisk together all of the ingredients for the marinade in a medium mixing bowl.
2. Add chicken to mixing bowl and toss to coat.
3. Cover and refrigerate 2 hours or overnight.
4. Preheat grill to medium high heat and brush with olive oil.
5. Thread the chicken strips onto metal skewers.
6. Place the chicken skewers on the prepared grill and cook 3 minutes, rotate, and grill another 4 minutes or until the chicken is cooked through.
7. Whisk together all of the ingredients for the almond butter sauce in a small saucepan.
8. Bring the sauce to a boil on medium heat, then lower to medium low and simmer for 1 to 2 minutes or until the sauce thickens.
9. Serve chicken satay warm with the almond butter sauce and enjoy.

Nutritional Info: Calories: 347, Sodium: 743mg, Dietary Fiber: 1.2g, Fat: 19.7 g, Carbs: 8.6g, Protein: 34.3g.

TEQUILA-GLAZED GRILLED CHICKEN THIGHS

SERVINGS: 4 - 6

Prep time: 10 minutes
Cook time: 20 minutes

INGREDIENTS

6 boneless, skinless chicken thighs
For the chicken seasoning:
1-1/2 teaspoon ground cumin
1 teaspoon chili powder
3/4 teaspoon kosher salt
1/4 teaspoon chipotle chile powder

FOR THE GLAZE:

3/4 cup pineapple juice
1/3 cup tequila
1/4 cup honey
2 teaspoon cornstarch
2 teaspoon water
2 teaspoon lime zest
3 tablespoon fresh lime juice
1/4 teaspoon crushed red pepper
Non-stick cooking spray

Tequila-Glazed Grilled Chicken Thighs are a delicious way to serve up a quick and hearty meal any night of the week. Serve them with rice and fajita veggies or even a delicious side of black beans and grilled vegetables. No matter how you pair this chicken, it will soon become a grill favorite.

DIRECTIONS

1. Preheat grill to medium-high heat using both burners. After preheating, turn the left burner off and leave the right burner on.
2. Combine the chicken seasoning in a small bowl and rub evenly over chicken.
3. Bring the pineapple juice, tequila, and honey to a boil in a small saucepan; cook until reduced to 3/4 cup; about 10 minutes.
4. Whisk cornstarch and 2 teaspoons of water in a small bowl until smooth.
5. Add cornstarch mixture to juice mixture and whisk into a boil; cook for 1 minute, stirring constantly.
6. Remove from heat and fold in red pepper, lime zest and 3 tablespoons lime juice.
7. Spray grill with non-stick cooking spray.
8. Add chicken to grill and cook 7 minutes on each side, basting with glaze often.
9. Move the chicken over to the left burner on indirect heat. Tent with foil and cook an additional 5 minutes on each side or until done, basting occasionally.
10. Serve warm with your favorite sides.

Nutritional Info: Calories: 381, Sodium: 425mg, Dietary Fiber: 0.5g, Fat: 11.1g, Carbs: 19g, Protein: 42.7g.

ROOT BEER CAN CHICKEN

SERVINGS: 2 - 4

Prep time: 8 hours 10 minutes
Cook time: 20 minutes

INGREDIENTS

1 lb. boneless chicken thighs
3 (12 ounce) cans root beer, like A&W
Olive oil

FOR THE RUB:

1 tablespoon garlic powder
3/4 tablespoon sea salt
1/2 tablespoon white pepper
2 teaspoons smoked paprika
2 teaspoons garlic powder
1 teaspoon dried thyme
1/8 teaspoon cayenne pepper

A take on the traditional grilled root beer can chicken, this dish is just as delicious as the whole roasted version and packed with savory sweet flavor. Believe it or not, you can enjoy this scrumptious dish with mashed potatoes, a warm beet salad, roasted Brussel sprouts, and a delicious Malbec or Shiraz for one very romantic meal.

DIRECTIONS

1. Combine rub ingredients in a bowl; reserve half in a separate air tight container until ready to grill.
2. Rub chicken thighs evenly with olive oil and coat each with some rub.
3. Lay chicken in a 13 by 9 inch baking dish. Cover with 2 cans of root beer.
4. Preheat grill to medium-high heat.
5. Discard marinade and brush grill with olive oil.
6. Gently fold remaining rub and a half of the third can of root beer in a small bowl.
7. Grill chicken for 7 minutes on each side, basting often with root beer rub mix.
8. Serve when cooked through or chicken reaches 165°F and juices run clear.

Nutritional Info: Calories: 363, Sodium: 1185mg, Dietary Fiber: 0.9g, Fat: 12.1 g, Carbs: 29.9g, Protein: 33.4g.

BASIL, BLACKBERRY, AND GRILLED CHICKEN SALAD

SERVINGS: 2

Prep time: 10 minutes
Cook time: 20 minutes

A breath of fresh air, this salad will transform your healthy lifestyle into one with robust flavors! You'll love this delicious recipe with a glass of sparkling water or iced tea.

INGREDIENTS

2 boneless, skinless chicken breasts,
1/4 cup extra-virgin olive oil, divided
3/4 teaspoon kosher salt, divided
1/2 teaspoon black pepper, divided
2 tablespoons white balsamic vinegar
1-1/2 teaspoons honey
1-1/2 teaspoons Dijon mustard
4 cups baby spinach
2 cups fresh basil, stems removed
1/4 cup red onion, super-thinly sliced
1 punnet fresh blackberries
1/2 cup goat cheese, crumbled
Cooking spray

DIRECTIONS

1. Preheat grill to medium-high.
2. Brush chicken with 1 tablespoon olive oil and sprinkle evenly with 1/4 teaspoon salt and 1/4 teaspoon pepper.
3. Spray grill with non-stick cooking spray, add chicken, and cook 5 minutes on each side or until the meat thermometer inserted in thickest portion registers 165°F.
4. Allow to rest for 5 minutes and cut into slices.
5. Whisk remaining 3 tablespoons oil, vinegar, honey, mustard, remaining 1/2 teaspoon salt, and remaining 1/4 teaspoon pepper together in a large mixing bowl. Add spinach, basil, and onion; toss gently to coat.
6. Divide salad evenly amongst 2 plates; top evenly with chicken, blackberries, and cheese to serve.

Nutritional Info: Calories: 607, Sodium: 1116mg, Dietary Fiber: 6,1g, Fat: 39.7g, Carbs: 16.2g, Protein: 48.3g.

HONEY SRIRACHA GRILLED CHICKEN THIGHS

SERVINGS: 6

Prep: 5 minutes
Cook time: 35 minutes

INGREDIENTS

2.5 lbs. boneless chicken thighs

3 tablespoons butter, unsalted

1 tablespoon fresh ginger, minced

2 garlic cloves, minced

1/4 teaspoon smoked paprika

1/4 teaspoon chili powder

4 tablespoons honey

3 tablespoons Sriracha

1 tablespoon lime juice

Spicy sweet chicken thighs are not only super-tasty, but super-easy to whip up even when you are pressed for time. Simply marinate overnight and throw them on the grill after work for a quick and easy restaurant quality meal right at home.

DIRECTIONS

1. Preheat grill to medium high.
2. Melt butter in a small saucepan on medium low heat; when melted add ginger and garlic. Stir until fragrant, about 2 minutes.
3. Fold in smoked paprika, ground cloves, honey, Sriracha and lime juice. Stir to combine, turn heat to medium and simmer for 5 minutes.
4. Rinse and pat chicken thighs dry.
5. Season with salt and pepper on both sides.
6. Spray grill with non-stick cooking spray.
7. Place chicken thighs on grill, skin side down first. Grill for 5 minutes. Flip the chicken over and grill on the other side for 5 minutes.
8. Continue to cook chicken, flipping every 3 minutes, so it doesn't burn, until the internal temperature reads 165°F on a meat thermometer.
9. During the last 5 minutes of grilling brush the glaze on both sides of the chicken.
10. Remove from grill and serve warm.

Nutritional Info: Calories: 375, Sodium: 221mg, Dietary Fiber: 0.3g, Fat: 22.5g, Carbs: 14.7g, Protein: 32g.

CHAPTER 5

MAIN DISHES: BEEF

CAPRESE FLANK STEAK

SERVINGS: 4

Prep time: 10 minutes
Cook time: 10 minutes

INGREDIENTS

4 (6 ounce) flank steaks

Sea salt, for seasoning

Flaky sea salt, for serving

Fresh ground pepper

Olive oil, Premium brand like Partanna

2 Roma tomatoes, sliced

4 ounces fresh buffalo mozzarella, cut into four slices

8 fresh basil leaves

Balsamic vinegar glaze, for drizzling

A super-fresh take on steak, this recipe elevates the delicious flank cut of steak to a whole new level. Best served with grilled eggplant, salad, pasta and a glass of Sangiovese for one decadent, Italian-inspired meal.

DIRECTIONS

1. Lightly brush each filet, on all sides, with olive oil and season with salt and pepper.
2. Preheat grill to high. Place steaks on grill, reduce heat to medium, tent with foil and cook for 5 minutes.
3. Flip, re-tent, and cook for an additional 5 minutes; during the last 2 minutes of grilling top each with a slice of mozzarella.
4. Remove steaks from the grill and top each with a few tomato slices, 2 basil leafs,
5. Drizzle with balsamic glaze, and sprinkle with flaky salt and a little more black pepper.

Nutritional Info: Calories: 461, Sodium: 485mg, Dietary Fiber: 0.8g, Fat: 22.8g, Carbs: 5.7g, Protein: 55.9g.

TENDER STEAK WITH PINEAPPLE RICE

SERVINGS: 4

Prep time: 10 minutes
Cook time: 10 minutes

INGREDIENTS

4 (4-ounce) beef fillets

1/4 cup soy sauce

1/2 teaspoon black pepper

1/2 teaspoon garlic powder

1 (8-ounce) can pineapple chunks, in juice, drained

2 scallions, thin sliced

2 (8.8-ounce) packages pre-cooked brown rice, like Uncle Ben's

7/8 teaspoon kosher salt

Olive oil, for brushing

Sticky, sweet pineapple rice is one delicious compliment to tender grilled steak. You'll definitely impress family and friends with this yummy recipe when you serve it with grilled veggies and iced green tea.

DIRECTIONS

1. Combine soy sauce, pepper, garlic powder, and beef in a large sealable plastic bag.
2. Seal and massage sauce into beef; let stand at room temperature for 7 minutes, turning bag occasionally.
3. Preheat grill to medium-high heat and brush with olive oil.
4. Add pineapple and green onions to grill and cook 5 minutes or until well charred, turning to char evenly.
5. Remove pineapple mix and brush with additional olive oil.
6. Add steaks and cook 3 minutes on each side, for rare, or until desired temperature is reached.
7. Cook rice according to package instructions.
8. Add rice, pineapple, onions, and salt to a bowl and stir gently to combine.
9. Plate steaks with pineapple rice and serve!

Nutritional Info: Calories: 369, Sodium: 1408mg, Dietary Fiber: 2.1g, Fat: 12.4g, Carbs: 37g, Protein: 27.9g.

RIB-EYE STEAK WITH HERBED STEAK BUTTER

SERVINGS: 2 - 4

Prep time: 12 hours
Cook time: 50 minutes

INGREDIENTS

1 (24-ounce) bone-in Tomahawk rib-eye, about 2-1/2 inches thick

Olive oil

Sea salt

Fresh Cracked pepper

3 tablespoons premium French butter

1/2 teaspoon Herbes de Provence

Grilled rib-eye is one tender, delicious way to enjoy steak - especially topped with creamy, herbed French butter. Decadent meets succulent in this grilling combination of perfectly blended flavors. Serve with mashed potatoes and the grilled asparagus recipe below for one delicious meal.

DIRECTIONS

1. Beat butter with herbs in a small mixing bowl, cover and refrigerate until ready to grill rib-eye.
2. Rub the rib-eye liberally with olive oil, salt and pepper until entire steak is covered.
3. Wrap lightly with cling wrap and place in the refrigerator to marinate for 12 hours.
4. Preheat the grill to high heat on one side and medium low on the other side, at least one hour prior to cooking.
5. Remove the steak from the refrigerator and leave at room temperature during the hour that the grill is preheating.
6. Place the steak on the center of the hottest side of the grill and rotate left and right to get proper grill marks. Do this for both sides, about 10 minutes.
7. Move the rib-eye to the cooler side of the grill and cook to rare, about 25 to 30 minutes.
8. Transfer rib-eye to a grill rack, add herbed butter on top, and lightly tent it with tin foil to rest for at least 15 minutes before carving.
9. Serve with your favorite sides!

Nutritional Info: Calories: 549, Sodium: 607mg, Dietary Fiber: 1.5g, Fat: 40.3g, Carbs: 3.5g, Protein: 40.9g.

HIGH-LOW STRIP STEAK

SERVINGS: 2

Prep time: 8 - 12 hours
Cook time: 15 minutes

INGREDIENTS

2 (1-pound) New York strip steaks, trimmed

FOR THE RUB:

1 bunch thyme sprigs

1 bunch rosemary sprigs

1 bunch sage sprigs

1-1/2 teaspoons black pepper, divided

3/4 teaspoon sea salt, divided

1/2 teaspoon garlic powder

2 tablespoons chopped fresh flat-leaf parsley

2 tablespoons extra-virgin olive oil

FOR THE BASTING LIQUID:

1/4 cup extra-virgin olive oil

1 tablespoon onion powder

1 tablespoon chopped fresh thyme

1 tablespoon sugar

1 teaspoon butter, unsalted

1 teaspoon Worcestershire sauce

1/2 teaspoon freshly ground black pepper

1/4 teaspoon kosher salt

1/4 teaspoon crushed red pepper

High-low strip steaks are the perfect way to quickly grill up a delicious NY Strip steak. Scrumptiously seasoned these steaks pair deliciously with creamy mashed potatoes and grilled asparagus.

DIRECTIONS

1. Combine basting liquid ingredients in a saucepan and bring to a simmer over medium heat. Remove from heat; refrigerate in an airtight container overnight.
2. Preheat grill to high heat.
3. Combine rub ingredients in a small mixing bowl and rub steaks with spice mixture; let rest 10 minutes.
4. Combine basting liquid ingredients in a small mixing bowl; reserve half for serving.
5. Place steaks on grill and cook 1 minute per side; baste with basting liquid frequently.
6. Turn grill down to medium heat.
7. Turn steaks and grill 3 additional minutes per side; or until thermometer registers 135°F for medium rare.
8. Remove steaks to a platter; baste with basting liquid using herb brush. Let stand 15 minutes.
9. Let rest 5 minutes. Cut steaks across grain into thin slices.
10. Serve steaks with reserved basting liquid.

Nutritional Info: Calories: 755, Sodium: 1374 mg, Dietary Fiber: 2.5g, Fat: 32.4g, Carbs: 13.7g, Protein: 102.7g.

GREEK FLANK STEAK GYROS

SERVINGS: 4

Prep Time: 5 minutes
Cook Time: 20 minutes

Grilled flank steak makes for the perfect protein to stuff inside warmed pita pockets. When you're craving a taste of Greece be sure to serve this alongside hummus and carrots with a glass of sparkling water and lemon.

INGREDIENTS

- 1 pound flank steak
- 1 white onion, thinly sliced
- 1 Roma tomato, thinly sliced
- 1 cucumber, peeled and thinly sliced
- 1/4 cup crumbled feta cheese
- 4 6-inch pita pockets

FOR THE MARINADE:

- 1/4 cup olive oil, plus more for brushing
- 1 teaspoon dried oregano
- 1 teaspoon balsamic vinegar
- 1 teaspoon garlic powder
- Sea salt and freshly ground pepper, to taste

FOR THE SAUCE:

- 1 cup plain yogurt
- 2 tablespoons fresh dill (can use dried), chopped
- 1 teaspoon garlic, minced
- 2 tablespoons lemon juice

DIRECTIONS

1. Cut the flank steak into thin strips against the grain. Add the marinade ingredients to a large sealable plastic bag, add the sliced meat, seal, and turn to coat.
2. Place in the refrigerator to marinate for 2 hours or overnight.
3. Preheat the grill to medium-high heat, and an oven to 250 degrees Fahrenheit.
4. Combine the sauce ingredients in small mixing bowl and set aside.
5. Spritz the pitas with a little water, wrap in foil and place in the oven to warm.
6. Brush grill with olive oil.
7. Add meat to grill and discard marinade. Cook until brown and cooked through, about 5 minutes.
8. Remove the pitas from the oven, and cut in half.
9. Arrange the pitas on plates and stuff with cucumber, tomato, onions, and beef.
10. Spoon some yogurt sauce over the meat and top with feta and serve.

Nutritional Info: Calories: 901, Sodium: 1221mg, Dietary Fiber: 5.7g, Fat: 27.2g, Carbs: 107.8g, Protein: 53.5g.

COFFEE AND BROWN SUGAR-CRUSTED SKIRT STEAK WITH GRILLED OKRA AND JALAPEÑOS

SERVINGS: 8

Prep time: 10 minutes
Cook time: 20 minutes

INGREDIENTS

1/4 cup espresso, finely ground

1/4 cup dark brown sugar, firmly packed

1-1/2 teaspoon sea salt

1/8 teaspoon ground cinnamon

1/8 teaspoon ground ginger

1/8 teaspoon ground white pepper

1/8 teaspoon five-spice powder

Pinch cayenne pepper

2-1/2 lb. skirt steak, cut into 4 pieces

1 tablespoon olive oil

Serve up something delicious for dinner when you grill up skirt steak with okra and jalapenos. You'll love this recipe served with a side of brown rice and a glass of Malbec or sparkling water.

DIRECTIONS

1. Heat grill to high.
2. Combine coffee, brown sugar, salt, cinnamon, ginger, white pepper, five-spice powder, and cayenne pepper in a bowl.
3. Remove steak from refrigerator and let come to room temperature, about 15 minutes. Rub steak with oil, and sprinkle with rub. Massage rub into meat.
4. Grill until charred and medium-rare, 2 to 4 minutes per side. Transfer to a cutting board, cover with foil and let rest 5 minutes before thinly slicing at an angle. Serve immediately.

Nutritional Info: Calories: 324, Sodium: 461mg, Dietary Fiber: 0.1g, Fat: 16g, Carbs: 4.6g, Protein: 37.9g.

COFFEE-RUBBED TEXAS-STYLE BRISKET

SERVINGS: 6

Prep time: 10 minutes
Cook time: 6 hours 20 minutes

INGREDIENTS

1 (4-1/2 lb) flat cut beef brisket (about 3 inches thick)

FOR THE RUB:

1 tablespoon ground coffee

1 tablespoon sea salt

1 tablespoon dark brown sugar

2 teaspoons smoked paprika

2 teaspoons chili powder

1 teaspoon garlic powder

1 teaspoon onion powder

1 teaspoon ground black pepper

1 teaspoon mesquite liquid smoke, like Colgin

Coffee makes for a decadent rub when it comes to seasoning juicy steak to perfection. Slow cooked on low heat all day, you'll love making this for your next backyard barbecue or family fun day at home.

DIRECTIONS

1. Combine the rub ingredients in a small mixing bowl.
2. Rinse and pat brisket dry and rub with coffee mix.
3. Preheat the grill for indirect grilling; heat one side to high and leaving one side with low heat.
4. Sear on high heat side for 3 - 5 minutes on each side or until nicely charred.
5. Move to low heat side, tent with foil, and cook for 6 hours or until a meat thermometer registers 195°.
6. Remove from grill. Let stand, covered, 30 minutes.
7. Cut brisket across grain into thin slices and serve.

Nutritional Info: Calories: 591, Sodium: 3953mg, Dietary Fiber: 0.7g, Fat: 42.8g, Carbs: 3.2g, Protein: 45.9g.

MEXICAN GRILLED STEAK SALAD

SERVINGS: 2

Prep time: 10 minutes
Cook time: 10 minutes

INGREDIENTS

STEAK MARINADE:

2 tablespoons olive oil

3 garlic cloves, minced

2 teaspoons chili powder

1 teaspoon ground cumin

1 teaspoon kosher salt

1 teaspoon freshly ground pepper

1-1/2 pounds skirt or flap steak, cut into 4-inch lengths

1/2 cup lager beer

SALAD:

12 ounces romaine hearts, trimmed and chopped

1 can black beans, drained and rinsed

1 pint cherry tomatoes, halved

1 large ripe avocado, pitted, peeled, and cut into chunks

About 1/3 cup crumbled queso fresco

Chopped fresh cilantro, for garnish

Kosher salt

DRESSING:

1 large ripe avocado, pitted, peeled, and cut into chunks

1/2 cup plain, whole-milk Greek yogurt

1/3 cup chopped fresh cilantro

Zest of 1 lime

Juice of 2 limes

Juicy steak is the perfect way to top a Mexican-inspired salad. Spice meets creamy avocado dressing for a healthy way to enjoy steak for both lunch and dinner!

DIRECTIONS

1. Lightly brush each steak, on all sides, with olive oil and season with salt and pepper.
2. Preheat grill to high. Place steaks on grill, reduce heat to medium, tent with foil and cook for 5 minutes.
3. Flip, re-tent, and cook for an additional 5 minutes.
4. Remove steaks from the grill, and slice into strips.
5. Mix salad ingredients together in large bowl. Place steak strips on top.
6. Mix dressing ingredients together in small bowl and drizzle over steak strips and salad.

Nutritional Info: Calories: 1332, Sodium: 2011mg, Dietary Fiber: 13.3g, Fat: 65.1g, Carbs: 29.4g, Protein: 152.3g.

GRILLED STEAKS WITH SWEET-SPICY HOISIN SAUCE

SERVINGS: 6

Prep time: 15 minutes
Cook time: 35 minutes

INGREDIENTS

6 (8 ounce) NY strip steaks

2 large sweet onions, sliced crosswise 1/2 inch thick

Sea salt and fresh ground black pepper

1/4 cup olive oil, plus more for rubbing

4 medium shallots, thinly sliced

4 garlic cloves, minced

1 tablespoon finely grated ginger

1/2 teaspoon crushed red pepper

1/3 cup chopped cilantro

1/3 cup hoisin sauce

3 tablespoons soy sauce

1/2 cup chicken stock

3 tablespoons honey

3 tablespoons unsalted butter

Sweet and spicy hoisin sauce is the perfect compliment to a delicious NY strip steak. Serve this delicious steak with brown rice, your favorite flash grilled veggies, and iced green tea for a delicious, quick Asian-inspired meal.

DIRECTIONS

1. Preheat grill to medium-high.
2. Heat the oil, shallots, garlic, ginger, crushed red pepper and cilantro in a saucepan over medium heat, stirring occasionally, until softened, about 7 minutes.
3. Add the hoisin, soy sauce and chicken stock, raise the heat to medium-high and boil until thickened, about 5 minutes.
4. Fold in the honey.
5. Remove from heat and stir in the butter until well-blended; keep warm.
6. Generously rub the steaks and onions with olive oil and season with salt and pepper.
7. Grill the steaks for 4 minutes per side.
8. Transfer the steaks to a carving board and let rest for 5 minutes.
9. Grill the onions for 4 minutes per side, or until charred. Transfer the onions to a plate.
10. Serve steaks with onions, hoisin sauce, and your favorite sides.

Nutritional Info: Calories: 703, Sodium: 3536mg, Dietary Fiber: 1.8g, Fat: 38.9g, Carbs: 22.8g, Protein: 63.5g.

GREEK FETA & SPINACH BURGERS

SERVINGS: 2

Prep time: 25 minutes
Cook time: 8 minutes

INGREDIENTS

1/2 pound lean ground beef

2 tablespoons crumbled reduced-fat feta cheese

1 clove garlic, minced

1/8 teaspoon ground black pepper

1 whole wheat hamburger bun, split and toasted

2 teaspoons tzatziki, for garnish

1/2 cup fresh spinach leaves, for garnish

2 tomato slices, for garnish

Sliced red onion, for garnish

Turn your favorite burgers into a Greek feast with these decadently stuffed burgers. You'll love this served with turnip fries and hummus!

DIRECTIONS

1. In a medium bowl combine ground beef, feta cheese, garlic, and pepper. Shape mixture into two 1/2-inch-thick patties.
2. Preheat grill to medium-high heat and cook for 4 minutes, flip, and cook 4 more minutes; or until an instant-read thermometer inserted patties reads 160 degrees Fahrenheit.
3. Spread tzatziki on each bun top. Line bun with spinach. Top bottom bun with burgers.
4. Top burger with tomato slices, red onion, then the spinach lined bun top and serve.

Nutritional Info: Calories: 377, Sodium: 493mg, Dietary Fiber: 3.2g, Fat: 12.8g, Carbs: 17.7g, Protein: 42.3g.

TUSCAN-STYLE STEAK WITH CRISPY POTATOES

SERVINGS: 4

Prep time: 30 minutes
Cook time: 35 minutes

INGREDIENTS

2 bone-in porterhouse steaks

1-1/2 lb. small potatoes, like Yukon Gold, scrubbed but skins left on, halved

4 tablespoons extra-virgin olive oil, divided

Sea salt and freshly ground pepper, to taste

2 teaspoons red wine, like Sangiovese or Montepulciano

1 teaspoon balsamic vinegar

pinch red pepper flakes

3 fresh rosemary sprigs, needles removed (discard stems)

Sweet and savory, this recipe calls for an Italian twist on classic meat and potatoes you'll absolutely love.

DIRECTIONS

1. Add potatoes to a large pot and cover with water, bring to a boil over high heat, then reduce the heat to medium-high and cook until the potatoes are almost tender, about 10 minutes. Drain, add to a medium mixing bowl, coat with 2 tablespoons olive oil, and set aside.
2. Preheat grill to medium heat.
3. Whisk 2 tablespoons olive oil, rosemary needles, red wine, vinegar, and pepper flakes; add steaks to marinade and set aside until ready to grill.
4. Sprinkle potatoes with salt and pepper.
5. Add steaks to one side of the grill and potatoes to the other.
6. Cook steak for 5 minutes, flip and 4 minutes on the other side for medium rare.
7. Add the potatoes to cook for 5 minutes.
8. Transfer steaks to a cutting board and tent with aluminum foil and let rest for 5 minutes while potatoes are cooking.
9. Divide each steak into 2 pieces and divide among 4 dinner plates. Spoon some potatoes around the steak and serve hot!

Nutritional Info: Calories: 366, Sodium: 153 mg, Dietary Fiber: 4.5g, Fat: 23.3g, Carbs: 27.3g, Protein: 13.4g.

CAPRESE GRILLED FILET MIGNON

SERVINGS: 4

Prep time: 10 minutes
Cook time: 10 minutes

INGREDIENTS

4 (6 ounce) filets

1 teaspoon garlic salt

Italian Olive oil

2 Roma tomatoes, sliced

4 ounces fresh buffalo mozzarella, cut into four slices

8 fresh basil leaves

Balsamic vinegar glaze, for drizzling

Sea salt, for seasoning

Fresh ground pepper

Serve up something healthy, with these tender fillets topped with a taste of the Mediterranean. Serve with creamy risotto, succulent grilled scallops and your favorite red wine for a surf and turf dream meal right at home.

DIRECTIONS

1. Lightly brush each filet, on all sides, with olive oil and rub with garlic salt.
2. Preheat grill to high. Place steaks on grill, reduce heat to medium, tent with foil and cook for 5 minutes.
3. Flip, re-tent, and cook for an additional 5 minutes; during the last 2 minutes of grilling top each with a slice of mozzarella.
4. Remove steaks from the grill and top each with a few tomato slices, 2 basil leafs,
5. Drizzle with balsamic, sprinkle with sea salt and black pepper and serve.

Nutritional Info: Calories: 406, Sodium: 688mg, Dietary Fiber: 0.8g, Fat: 21.8g, Carbs: 7.2g, Protein: 45.1g.

FLANK STEAK WITH GARLIC AND ROSEMARY

SERVINGS: 4

Prep time: 10 minutes
Cook time: 20 minutes

INGREDIENTS

2 (8 ounce) flank steaks

FOR THE MARINADE:

1 tablespoon extra virgin olive oil, plus more for brushing

2 tablespoons fresh rosemary, chopped

4 cloves garlic, minced

2 teaspoons sea salt

1/4 teaspoon black pepper

Flavorful and delicious, the flank steak is perfect complimented with robust garlic and spicy rosemary. Serve on top of a bed or your favorite greens dressed with balsamic vinegar and olive oil for one very healthy meal.

DIRECTIONS

1. Add marinade ingredients to a food processor or blender and pulse until garlic and rosemary are pulverized.
2. Use a fork to pierce the steaks 10 times on each side.
3. Rub each evenly with the marinade on both sides.
4. Place in a covered dish and refrigerate for at least 1 hour or overnight.
5. Preheat grill to high and brush with olive oil and preheat to high.
6. Cook steaks for 5 minutes, flip, tent with foil, and cook for about 3-4 minutes more.
7. Transfer meat to rest on a cutting board, cover with aluminum foil, for about 15 minutes.
8. Slice very thin against the grain and serve immediately.

Nutritional Info: Calories: 737, Sodium: 1001mg, Dietary Fiber: 0.8g, Fat: 13.2g, Carbs: 2.1g, Protein: 31.8g.

BEEF PINWHEELS

SERVINGS: 4 - 8

Prep time: 10 minutes
Cook time: 8 minutes

INGREDIENTS

1 pound Sirloin,

cut into 4-1/2 inches thick pieces

1 tablespoon salt

Olive oil, for rubbing pinwheels

Freshly ground pepper

FOR THE STUFFING:

1 jar red pesto

2 tablespoons pancetta

1 clove garlic

Beef Pinwheels are a delicious way to serve up something different. Great for dinner parties, this appetizer can be served on a bed of arugula tossed in lemon juice or all on its very own.

DIRECTIONS

1. Preheat grill to medium-high heat.
2. Presoak a dozen toothpicks in warm water.
3. Add stuffing ingredients to a food processor or blender and pulse until well-combined.
4. Pound out the sirloin pieces until super-thin.
5. Season the sirloin pieces generously with oil, salt and pepper.
6. Spoon stuffing on top of each of the pieces.
7. Roll up like a jelly-roll and secure on either end with soaked toothpicks.
8. Grill the pinwheels for 3 to 4 minutes per side, rotating to evenly cook.
9. Allow to rest for 5 minutes and serve.

Nutritional Info: Calories: 363, Sodium: 1643mg, Dietary Fiber: 1.7g, Fat: 25.3g, Carbs: 1.7g, Protein: 29.6g.

CARNE ASADA

SERVINGS: 4

Prep time: 1 - 2 hours
Cook time: 15 minutes

INGREDIENTS

1 lb. arrachera or hanger steak, sliced thin

1/4 cup olive oil

1 lime, juiced

1 orange, juiced

1 garlic clove, finely chopped

1/2 teaspoon cumin

1/4 teaspoon salt

1/4 teaspoon ground pepper

Handful of fresh cilantro, chopped

Grill up a taste of Mexico with this delicious Carne Asada recipe. Charred steak, seasoned to perfection can be served as a main dish or as the ingredient in several of your favorite Mexican inspired meals like tacos and burritos.

DIRECTIONS

1. Combine all of the ingredients in a large sealable plastic bag. Marinate in the refrigerator for 1 to 2 hours.
2. Preheat to medium/high heat, grill for 2 minutes on each side or until just cooked through.
3. Transfer to cutting board to rest for 10 minutes.
4. Slice against the grain and serve.

Nutritional Info: Calories: 363, Sodium: 200mg, Dietary Fiber: 1.7g, Fat: 18.4g, Carbs: 7.7g, Protein: 41.6g.

BASIC JUICY NY STRIP STEAK

SERVINGS: 1

Prep time: 45 minutes
Cook time: 8 minutes

INGREDIENTS

1 (8 ounce) NY strip steak
Olive oil
Sea salt
Fresh ground black pepper

When you are craving a basic, juicy steak with no frills - this is the recipe to try out on you gas grill. Simple and succulent, this steak is for those who love bare bones seasoning without sacrificing flavor.

DIRECTIONS

1. Remove the steak from the refrigerator and let it come to room temperature, about 30 to 45 minutes.
2. Preheat grill to medium-high heat and brush with olive oil.
3. Season the steak on all sides with salt and pepper.
4. Cook steak about 4 to 5 minutes.
5. Flip and cook about 4 minutes more for medium rare steak; between 125°F and 130°F on a meat thermometer.
6. Transfer the steak to a plate and let it rest for 5 minutes before serving.

Nutritional Info: Calories: 1560, Sodium: 8468mg, Dietary Fiber: 0g, Fat: 86g, Carbs: 0.1g, Protein: 184g.

RIB EYE STEAK WITH ROMAINE MARMALADE AND WATERCRESS

SERVINGS: 6

Prep time: 10 minutes
Cook time: 40 minutes

INGREDIENTS

STEAK:

One 24-ounce bone-in rib eye chop, about 2-1/2 inches thick

Extra virgin olive oil

Flaky sea salt

Cracked pepper

ROMAINE MARMALADE AND WATERCRESS:

4 bunches organic watercress, stems removed

2 whole leaves romaine lettuce, chopped

1 small clove garlic, minced

1/4 bunch fresh cilantro, trimmed and chopped fine

1/4 bunch fresh flat-leaf parsley, trimmed and chopped fine

1 lemon, juiced

1 teaspoon orange marmalade

Flakey sea salt, to taste

Fresh ground pepper, to taste

2 tablespoons extra-virgin olive oil

Crispy romaine meats tangy watercress and citrus sweet notes for an elevated way to serve a rib-eye. Easy to make, the whole family will love this bright steak served with iced tea or a crisp lager.

DIRECTIONS

1. Rub the rib-eye liberally with olive oil, salt and pepper until entire steak is covered.
2. Wrap lightly with cling wrap and place in the refrigerator to marinate for 12 hours.
3. Preheat the grill to high heat on one side and medium low on the other side, at least one hour prior to cooking.
4. Remove the steak from the refrigerator and leave at room temperature during the hour that the grill is preheating.
5. Combine romaine marmalade and watercress ingredients in a large mixing bowl and set aside.
6. Place the steak on the center of the hottest side of the grill and rotate left and right to get proper grill marks. Do this for both sides, about 10 minutes.
7. Move the rib-eye to the cooler side of the grill and cook to rare, about 25 to 30 minutes.
8. Transfer rib-eye to a grill rack, add romaine marmalade on top, and lightly tent it with tin foil to rest for at least 15 minutes before carving.
9. Serve with your favorite sides!

Nutritional Info: Calories: 293, Sodium: 271mg, Dietary Fiber: 1.1g, Fat: 8.6g, Carbs: 9g, Protein: 42.8g.

FLASH-MARINATED SKIRT STEAK

SERVINGS: 4

Prep time: 30 minutes
Cook time: 45 minutes

INGREDIENTS

2 (8 ounce) skirt steaks

FOR THE MARINADE:

2 tablespoons balsamic vinegar

2 teaspoons olive oil, more for brushing

2 garlic cloves, minced

Sea salt, to taste

Black pepper, to taste

Flash marinated flank steak is the perfect steak when you're pressed for time. Quick and easy to marinate, don't be afraid to prepare the recipe in the morning and cook it right after work!

DIRECTIONS

1. Combine marinade ingredients in a sealable plastic bag, add steaks, seal bag, turn to coat; let stand at room temperature for 30 minutes.
2. Preheat grill to medium-high heat.
3. Remove steaks and discard marinade, place on grill and cook about 3 minutes per side. Transfer steaks to cutting board and rest for 5 Minutes.
4. Cut across the grain into slices and serve with your favorite sides.

Nutritional Info: Calories: 256, Sodium: 204mg, Dietary Fiber: 0g, Fat: 13.8g, Carbs: 0.6g, Protein: 30.3g.

CHAPTER 6
MAIN DISHES: PORK

STICKY-SWEET PORK SHOULDER

SERVINGS: 6 - 8

Prep time: 8 hours
Cook time: 8 minutes

INGREDIENTS

1 (5 lbs.) Boston Butt pork shoulder

FOR THE MARINADE:

2 tablespoons garlic, minced

1 large piece ginger, peeled and chopped

1 cup hoisin sauce

3/4 cup fish sauce

2/3 cup honey

2/3 cup Shaoxing

1/2 cup chili oil

1/3 cup oyster sauce

1/3 cup sesame oil

FOR THE GLAZE:

3/4 cup dark brown sugar

1 tablespoon light molasses

Sweet and sticky sauce is the perfect compliment to savory grilled pork. Serve this delicious dish with your favorite sides or as a delicious stuffing for steamed buns or grilled bread.

DIRECTIONS

1. Place pork shoulder, fat side down, on a cutting board with a short end facing you. Holding a long sharp knife about 1"–1-1/2" above cutting board, make a shallow cut along the entire length of a long side of shoulder.

2. Continue cutting deeper into meat, lifting and unfurling with your free hand, until it lies flat.

3. Purée marinade in a blender and reserve 1-1/2 cups for glaze, cover and refrigerate.

4. Pour remaining marinade in a large sealable plastic bag.

5. Add pork shoulder to bag and marinate in the refrigerator for 8 hours.

6. Preheat grill to medium heat (with cover closed, thermometer should register 350°). Remove pork from marinade, letting excess drip off.

7. Add glaze ingredients to reserved marinade until sugar is dissolved.

8. Grill pork, for 8 minutes, basting and turning with tongs every minute or so, until thick coated with glaze, lightly charred in spots, and warmed through; an instant-read thermometer inserted into the thickest part should register 145°F.

9. Transfer to a cutting board and slice against the grain, 1/4" thick, to serve.

Nutritional Info: Calories: 1286, Sodium: 2875mg, Dietary Fiber: 1g, Fat: 84.8g, Carbs: 58.3g, Protein: 68.7g.

PINEAPPLE BACON PORK CHOPS

SERVINGS: 6

Prep time: 30 minutes
Cook time: 1 hour

INGREDIENTS

1 large whole pineapple

6 pork chops

12 slices thick-cut bacon

12 toothpicks, soaked in water for 1 hour

FOR THE GLAZE:

1/4 cup honey

1/8 teaspoon cayenne pepper

Sweet and juicy pineapple compliments savory pork for one incredible dish! You'll love the sweet and spicy kick in this dish - serve it with your favorite grilled side dishes and vegetables and a cold glass of beer or iced tea.

DIRECTIONS

1. Turn both burners to medium-high heat; after about 15 minutes, turn off one of the middle burners and turn the remaining burners down to medium.
2. Slice off the top and bottom of the pineapple, and peel the pineapple, cutting the skin off in strips.
3. Cut pineapple flesh into six quarters.
4. Wrap each pineapple section with a bacon slice; secure each end with a toothpick.
5. Brush quarters with honey and sprinkle with cayenne pepper.
6. Put the quarters on the griddle, flipping when bacon is cooked so that both sides are evenly grilled.
7. While pineapple quarters are cooking, coat pork chops with honey and cayenne pepper. Set on grill.
8. Tent with foil and cook for 1 hour, flipping half-way through. Chops should be cooked through and not pink.
9. Serve each chop with a pineapple quarter on the side.

Nutritional Info: Calories: 380, Sodium: 852mg, Dietary Fiber: 0.5g, Fat: 23.5g, Carbs: 18.2g, Protein: 25.8g.

HABANERO-MARINATED PORK CHOPS

SERVINGS: 4

Prep time: 30 minutes
Cook time: 13 minutes

INGREDIENTS

4-1/2 inches thick bone-in pork chops

3 tablespoons olive oil, plus more for grill

Kosher salt and freshly ground black pepper

FOR THE MARINADE:

1 habanero chile, seeded, chopped fine

2 garlic cloves, minced

1/2 cup fresh orange juice

2 tablespoons brown sugar

1 tablespoon apple cider vinegar

Kick things up a notch on your gas grill with this spicy recipe. These yummy pork chops pair perfectly with yellow rice, black beans, and your favorite salad.

DIRECTIONS

1. Combine marinade ingredients in a large sealable plastic bag.
2. Pierce pork chops all over with a fork and add to bag, seal, and turn to coat.
3. Marinate at room temperature, turning occasionally, for 30 minutes.
4. Prepare grill for medium-high heat.
5. Brush with oil.
6. Remove pork chops from marinade and pat dry.
7. Grill, turning occasionally, until charred and cooked through for 8 minutes.
8. Transfer to a plate and let rest 5 minutes.
9. Serve with your favorite sides.

Nutritional Info: Calories: 490, Sodium: 171mg, Dietary Fiber: 1.1g, Fat: 39.2g, Carbs: 10.9g, Protein: 23.3g.

MOROCCAN SPICED PORK TENDERLOIN WITH CREAMY HARISSA SAUCE

SERVINGS: 6

Prep: 40 minutes
Cook: 20 minutes

INGREDIENTS

2 (1 lb.) pork tenderloins
1 teaspoon ground cinnamon
1 teaspoon ground cilantro
1 teaspoon ground cumin
1 teaspoon paprika
1 teaspoon sea salt
2 tablespoons olive oil

FOR CREAMY HARISSA SAUCE:

1 cup Greek yogurt (8 ounces)
1 tablespoon fresh lemon juice
1 tablespoon extra-virgin olive oil
1 teaspoon harissa sauce
1 clove garlic, minced
Kosher salt and cracked black pepper

Moroccan spice and creamy harissa make for one delicious way to serve up tender pork any night of the week. Enjoy this yummy dish with collard greens and potato salad for a twist on your next cookout.

DIRECTIONS

1. Combine harissa ingredients in a small mixing bowl and set aside.
2. Combine the cinnamon, coriander, cumin, paprika, salt and olive oil.
3. Rub the seasonings evenly over the pork tenderloins; cover and refrigerate for 30 minutes.
4. Preheat grill to high-heat and cook tenderloins until browned; about 8 to 10 minutes.
5. Turn and cook an additional 8 to 10 minutes. Transfer the tenderloins to a cutting board, tent with foil and rest for 10 minutes.
6. Slice and serve with creamy harissa sauce.

Nutritional Info: Calories: 376, Sodium: 458mg, Dietary Fiber: 0.4g, Fat: 17.9g, Carbs: 2.6g, Protein: 48.7g.

PORK TENDERLOIN SANDWICHES

SERVINGS: 6

Prep time: 10 minutes
Cook time: 25 minutes

INGREDIENTS

2 (3/4-lb.) pork tenderloins

1 teaspoon garlic powder

1 teaspoon sea salt

1 teaspoon dry mustard

1/2 teaspoon coarsely ground pepper

Olive oil, for brushing

6 whole wheat hamburger buns

6 tablespoons barbecue sauce

Tender grilled pork is the perfect way to grill up a savory sandwich on your gas grill. This simple, yet flavorful sandwich will have you grilling like a gourmet chef in no time.

DIRECTIONS

1. Stir the garlic, salt, pepper, and mustard together in a small mixing bowl.
2. Rub pork tenderloins evenly with olive oil, then seasoning mix.
3. Preheat grill to medium-high heat, and cook 10 to 12 minutes on each side or until a meat thermometer inserted into thickest portion registers 155°F.
4. Remove from grill and let stand 10 minutes.
5. Slice thin and evenly pile onto hamburger buns.
6. Drizzle each sandwich with barbecue sauce and serve.

Nutritional Info: Calories: 372, Sodium: 694mg, Dietary Fiber: 2.9g, Fat: 13.4g, Carbs: 24.7g, Protein: 37.2g.

SWEET & SPICY BBQ RIBS

SERVINGS: 4 - 6

Prep time: 8 hours
Cook time: 1 hour

INGREDIENTS

2 Racks St Louis Style Ribs
2 bottles BBQ sauce, like Stubbs or Kraft

FOR THE RUB:

2 tablespoon paprika
1-1/2 tablespoon dark brown sugar
1 tablespoon garlic powder
1 tablespoon chili powder
1 tablespoon sea salt
1-1/2 teaspoon onion powder
1-1/2 teaspoon black pepper
1/2 teaspoon red chili flakes

Sweet and spicy ribs are a great way to grill out with the whole family on the weekends. Serve these sticky ribs with mashed potatoes and grilled vegetables for some decadent weekend backyard fun.

DIRECTIONS

1. Combine rub ingredients in a small mixing bowl; rub evenly over the ribs. Marinate overnight in refrigerator.
2. Preheat the oven to 300 degrees F. Place the ribs on a foil lined sheet pan, cover with foil and bake for an hour.
3. Baste the ribs, and continue to baste every 30-45 minutes; cook an additional 2 hours.
4. Remove the ribs from the oven, and baste them with more sauce.
5. Preheat grill to medium high.
6. Transfer ribs to grill and cook 10 minutes, basting regularly with the BBQ sauce.
7. Take them off, cover with foil, and let rest for 30 minutes.
8. Serve with your favorite sides.

Nutritional Info: Calories: 349, Sodium: 2112mg, Dietary Fiber: 2.4g, Fat: 13.1g, Carbs: 47.2g, Protein: 11.5g.

HERB-CRUSTED MEDITERRANEAN PORK TENDERLOIN

SERVINGS: 4

Prep time: 2 hours
Cook time: 30 minutes

INGREDIENTS

1 pound pork tenderloin

1 tablespoon olive oil

2 teaspoons dried oregano

3/4 teaspoon lemon pepper

1 teaspoon garlic powder

1/4 cup parmesan cheese, grated

3 tablespoons olive tapenade

Herb-Crusted Tenderloin with Mediterranean style spices is one great way to grill up juicy tenderloin. My favorite way to serve this dish is alongside lemon chili pasta and salad with a glass of Pinot Grigio.

DIRECTIONS

1. Place pork on large piece of plastic wrap.
2. Rub tenderloin with oil and sprinkle oregano, garlic powder, and lemon pepper evenly, over entire tenderloin.
3. Wrap tightly in the plastic wrap and refrigerate for 2 hours.
4. Preheat grill to medium-high heat.
5. Transfer pork to cutting board, remove plastic wrap, and make a lengthwise cut through center of tenderloin, open meat so it lies flat, but do not cut all the way through.
6. Combine tapenade and parmesan in a small mixing bowl; rub into the center of the tenderloin and fold meat back together.
7. Tie together with twine in 2-inch intervals.
8. Grill tenderloin for 20 minutes, turning tenderloin once during grilling, or until internal temperature reaches 145 degrees Fahrenheit.
9. Transfer tenderloin to cutting board.
10. Tent with foil; let rest for 10 minutes.
11. Remove string and cut into 1/4-inch-thick slices and serve.

Nutritional Info: Calories: 413, Sodium: 1279mg, Dietary Fiber: 0.5g, Fat: 30.5g, Carbs: 2.4g, Protein: 31.4g.

GRILLED PORK CHOPS WITH HERB APPLE COMPOTE

SERVINGS: 4

Prep time: 5 minutes
Cook time: 20 minutes

INGREDIENTS

4, bone-in pork chops

2 honeycrisp apples, peeled, cored and chopped

1/3 cup orange juice

1 teaspoon chopped fresh rosemary

1 teaspoon chopped fresh sage

Sea salt

Black pepper

Apples are one of my absolute favorites to pair with pork chops, and I hope you love this recipe too! Sweet meets juicy pork for a grilling flavor that is out of this world.

DIRECTIONS

1. Add the apples, herbs and orange juice to a saucepan and simmer over medium heat until the apples are tender and the juices are thickened to a syrup, about 10 to 12 minutes.
2. Season pork chops with salt and pepper.
3. Place on the grill and cook until the pork chop releases from the grill, about 4 minutes.
4. Flip and cook on the other side for 3 minutes.
5. Transfer to a cutting board and tent with foil.
6. Top with apple compote and serve!

Nutritional Info: Calories: 284, Sodium: 173mg, Dietary Fiber: 1g, Fat: 20g, Carbs: 7.2g, Protein: 18.2g.

DIJON HONEY PORK CHOPS WITH TOMATO-PEACH SALAD

SERVINGS: 4

Prep time: 10 minutes
Cook time: 25 minutes

INGREDIENTS

4 (8 ounce) bone-in pork chops

1/4 cups Dijon mustard

1/4 cup, plus 2 tablespoons red wine vinegar

2 tablespoons honey

8 tablespoon extra-virgin olive oil, divided

2 large heirloom tomatoes, cut into chunks

3 peaches, sliced

1/4 cup basil leaves, torn, plus more for garnish

Sea salt

Freshly ground black pepper

Transform your weeknight dinners with this delicious grilled pork chop recipe. Tangy Dijon mustard makes the perfect seasoning for juicy pork when served with a sweet salad on the side.

DIRECTIONS

1. Preheat an oven to 375°F. Place pork chops in a shallow glass baking dish.
2. Whisk together mustard, red wine vinegar, honey, and 4 tablespoons olive oil in a small mixing bowl.
3. Pour mixture over pork, turning to coat, and let rest 10 minutes.
4. Place tomatoes, peaches, and basil in a large mixing bowl.
5. Whisk together remaining 2 tablespoons vinegar and 4 tablespoons olive oil. Drizzle mixture over tomato-peach mixture and toss, and season with salt and pepper.
6. Heat grill to medium-high heat.
7. Remove pork chops from marinade and season with salt and pepper.
8. Grill 3 minutes per side, then transfer pan to oven and finish cooking for 6 minutes; or until the internal temperature reads 145°.
9. Let rest 5 minutes, and serve with tomato-peach salad and garnish with torn basil.

Nutritional Info: Calories: 1126, Sodium: 564mg, Dietary Fiber: 2.8g, Fat: 90.8g, Carbs: 24.1g, Protein: 55.3g.

HONEY SOY PORK CHOPS

SERVINGS: 6

Prep time: 1 hour
Cook time: 25 minutes

INGREDIENTS

6 (4 ounce) boneless pork chops

1/4 cup organic honey

1 to 2 tablespoons low sodium soy sauce

2 tablespoons olive oil

1 tablespoon rice mirin

Sweet and tangy grilled pork is absolutely delicious when grilled to perfection on your gas grill. Simply serve this dish with rice and grilled vegetables for one delicious meal.

DIRECTIONS

1. Combine honey, soy sauce, oil, and white vinegar and whisk until well-combined. Add sauce and pork chops to a large sealable plastic bag and marinate for 1 hour.
2. Preheat the grill to medium-high heat and cook for 4 to 5 minutes, or until the pork chop easily releases from the grill.
3. Flip and continue to cook for 5 additional minutes, or until internal temperature reaches 145 degrees Fahrenheit.
4. Serve and enjoy!

Nutritional Info: Calories: 251, Sodium: 187mg, Dietary Fiber: 0.1g, Fat: 8.7g, Carbs: 13.1g, Protein: 29.9g.

SWEET HEAT CHEERWINE BABY BACK RIBS

SERVINGS: 6 - 8

Prep time: 30 minutes
Cook time: 3 hours

INGREDIENTS

2 teaspoon smoked paprika

2 teaspoon chili powder

2 teaspoon dry mustard

1 teaspoon garlic powder

1 teaspoon ground ginger

2 (3 lb.) racks baby back ribs

1 (12-oz.) bottle Cheerwine soft drink

1 (15-oz.) can tomato sauce

1/3 cup light brown sugar

1 tablespoon Dijon mustard

1 teaspoon red chili flakes

Give baby back ribs a twist with sweet heat and serve these for your next backyard barbecue party. Serve with potato salad, baked beans, and crudité veggies for grilling fun.

DIRECTIONS

1. Preheat oven to 325°F.
2. Combine paprika, chili powder, dry mustard, garlic powder, and ginger in bowl. Sprinkle 2 tablespoons spice mixture over ribs, dividing evenly.
3. Place ribs on a baking sheet; wrap tightly with aluminum foil. Bake 2 hours.
4. Remove foil; rest 30 minutes.
5. Combine Cheerwine, tomato sauce, brown sugar, Dijon mustard, red pepper, and 1 tablespoon spice mixture in a medium saucepan. Bring to a boil over high heat.
6. Reduce heat and simmer, stirring occasionally, until reduced to 2 cups, about 25 to 30 minutes.
7. Heat grill to medium.
8. Grill ribs, basting with 1 cup of the sauce, turning frequently, until lightly charred and lacquered, about 10 to 15 minutes.
9. Transfer to a platter and serve with remaining sauce.

Nutritional Info: Calories: 1089, Sodium: 1492mg, Dietary Fiber: 1.5g, Fat: 56.1g, Carbs: 76.2g, Protein: 1.3g.

BIG JOHN'S CHILI-RUBBED RIBS

SERVINGS: 10

Prep time: 30 minutes
Cook time: 1 hour 30 minutes

INGREDIENTS

6 pounds baby back pork ribs

FOR THE RUB:

3 tablespoons brown sugar

2 tablespoons smoked paprika

2 tablespoons chili powder

3 teaspoons ground cumin

2 teaspoons garlic powder

1 teaspoon salt

FOR THE GLAZE:

1 cup reduced-sodium soy sauce

1 cup packed brown sugar

2/3 cup ketchup

1/3 cup lemon juice

1-1/2 teaspoons minced fresh ginger root

1/2 teaspoon red pepper flakes

Take your ribs to a whole new level with chili rub that is lip-smacking good. If you live dry rubbed, juicy ribs this is the recipe to whip up!

DIRECTIONS

1. Mix the rub ingredients and rub over ribs. Refrigerate, covered, for 30 minutes.
2. Wrap rib racks in aluminum foil and seal tightly.
3. Grill over indirect medium heat 1 to 1-1/2 hours or until tender.
4. Combine glaze ingredients in a saucepan and cook, uncovered, over medium heat for 8 minutes or until heated through and sugar is dissolved, stirring occasionally.
5. Remove ribs from foil.
6. Place ribs over direct heat; brush with the glaze.
7. Grill, covered, over medium heat 25 to 30 additional minutes or until browned, turning and brushing ribs occasionally with remaining glaze.
8. Serve hot!

Nutritional Info: Calories: 439, Sodium: 1382mg, Dietary Fiber: 1,5g, Fat: 33.1g, Carbs:11.4g, Protein: 23.9g.

GLAZED COUNTRY RIBS

SERVINGS: 6

Prep time: 10 minutes
Cook time: 4 hours

INGREDIENTS

- 3 pounds country-style pork ribs
- 1 cup low-sugar ketchup
- 1/2 cup water
- 1/4 cup onion, finely chopped
- 1/4 cup cider vinegar or wine vinegar
- 1/4 cup light molasses
- 2 tablespoons Worcestershire sauce
- 2 teaspoons chili powder
- 2 cloves garlic, minced

Country ribs are full of delicious flavor and make for one great main dish on weeknights or weekends with friends. Serve these ribs with your favorite sides and cold, crisp beer on summer days for traditional grilling fun.

DIRECTIONS

1. Combine ketchup, water, onion, vinegar, molasses, Worcestershire sauce, chili powder, and garlic in a saucepan and bring to boil; reduce heat. Simmer, uncovered, for 10 to 15 minutes or until desired thickness is reached, stirring often.
2. Trim fat from ribs.
3. Preheat grill to medium-high.
4. Place ribs, bone-side down, on grill and grill for 1-1/2 to 2 hours or until tender, brushing occasionally with sauce during the last 10 minutes of grilling.
5. Serve with remaining sauce and enjoy!

Nutritional Info: Calories: 404, Sodium: 733mg, Dietary Fiber: 0.4g, Fat: 8.1g, Carbs: 15.2g, Protein: 60.4g

YUCATAN-STYLE GRILLED PORK

SERVINGS: 4

Prep time: 15 minutes
Cook time: 8 minutes

INGREDIENTS

2 pork tenderloins, trimmed
1 teaspoon annatto powder
Olive oil

FOR THE MARINADE:

2 oranges, juiced
2 lemons, juiced, or more to taste
2 limes, juiced, or more to taste
6 cloves garlic, minced
1 teaspoon ground cumin
1/2 teaspoon cayenne pepper
1/2 teaspoon dried oregano
1/2 teaspoon black pepper

Elevate simple grilled pork with Yucatan citrus combinations to make something different on your gas grill. Serve this with a side of grilled plantains, veggies, and sparkling water.

DIRECTIONS

1. Combine marinade ingredients in a mixing bowl and whisk until well-blended.
2. Cut the tenderloins in half crosswise; cut each piece in half lengthwise.
3. Place pieces in marinade and thoroughly coat with the mixture.
4. Cover with plastic wrap and refrigerate 4 to 6 hours.
5. Transfer pieces of pork from marinade to a paper-towel-lined bowl to absorb most of the moisture.
6. Discard paper towels. Drizzle olive oil and a bit more annatto powder on the pork.
7. Preheat grill for medium-high heat and lightly oil.
8. Place pieces evenly spaced on grill; cook 4 to 5 minutes.
9. Turn and grill on the other side another 4 or 5 minutes.
10. Transfer onto a serving platter and allow meat to rest about 5 minutes before serving.

Nutritional Info: Calories: 439, Sodium: 1382mg, Dietary Fiber: 1.5g, Fat: 33.1g, Carbs: 11.4g, Protein: 23.9g.

SWEET SMOKED PORK RIBS

SERVINGS: 8 - 10

Prep time: 30 minutes
Cook time: 2 hours

INGREDIENTS

10 pounds baby back pork ribs

FOR THE RUB:

1 teaspoon liquid smoke, like Colgin

2 tablespoons packed brown sugar

2 tablespoons ground white pepper

2 tablespoons onion powder

1 tablespoon garlic powder

1 tablespoon chili powder

1 tablespoon smoked paprika

1 tablespoon cumin

FOR THE SAUCE:

1 cup apple juice

1/4 cup packed brown sugar

1/4 cup barbeque sauce

Sweet meets smoky and you get none other than ribs that will literally stick to yours! One of my favorite ways to grill ribs, you can serve this with just about anything and it's just plain delicious.

DIRECTIONS

1. Combine rub ingredients in a mixing bowl.
2. Rub the spice mixture into the baby back ribs on all sides.
3. Wrap the ribs well with plastic wrap, and refrigerate for at least 30 minutes prior to cooking.
4. Unwrap baby back ribs and place onto the wire racks of the smoker in a single layer.
5. Combine sauce ingredients in a saucepan and cook for 10 minutes.
6. Grill over indirect medium heat 1 to 1-1/2 hours or until tender.
7. Brush ribs with the glaze and grill, covered, over medium heat 25 to 30 additional minutes or until browned, turning and brushing ribs occasionally with remaining glaze.
8. Serve hot!

Nutritional Info: Calories: 1329, Sodium: 423mg, Dietary Fiber: 1.2g, Fat: 108.8g, Carbs: 10.5g, Protein: 73g.

CHAPTER 7
MAIN DISHES: SEAFOOD

GREMOLATA SWORDFISH SKEWERS

SERVINGS: 4

Prep time: 20 minutes
Cook time: 10 minutes

Delicate, flaky swordfish makes for one delicious grilled skewer! Serve your yummy swordfish with lemon chili pasta, salad, and Chardonnay or sparkling water with lemon.

INGREDIENTS

1-1/2 lb. skinless swordfish fillet

2 teaspoons lemon zest

3 tablespoons lemon juice

1/2 cup finely chopped parsley

2 teaspoon garlic, minced

3/4 teaspoon sea salt

1/4 teaspoon black pepper

2 tablespoons extra-virgin olive oil, plus extra for serving

1/2 teaspoon red pepper flakes

3 lemons, cut into slices

DIRECTIONS

1. Preheat grill to medium-high.
2. Combine lemon zest, parsley, garlic, 1/4 teaspoon of the salt, and pepper in a small bowl with a fork to make gremolata and set aside.
3. Mix swordfish pieces with reserved lemon juice, olive oil, red pepper flakes, and remaining salt.
4. Thread swordfish and lemon slices, alternating each, onto the metal skewers.
5. Grill skewers 8 to 10 minutes, flipping halfway through, or until fish is cooked through.
6. Place skewers on a serving platter and sprinkle with gremolata.
7. Drizzle with olive oil and serve.

Nutritional Info: Calories: 333, Sodium: 554mg, Dietary Fiber: 0.5g, Fat: 16g, Carbs: 1.6g, Protein: 43.7g.

SPICED SNAPPER WITH MANGO AND RED ONION SALAD

SERVINGS: 4

Prep time: 10 minutes
Cook time: 20 minutes

Spiced snapper meats cool, crisp mango salad for one delicious way to grill up lunch. Serve this gorgeous seafood feast with sparkling water with lemon and warm baguettes for a delicious lunch in the sun.

INGREDIENTS

2 red snappers, cleaned

Sea salt

1/3 cup tandoori spice

olive oil, plus more for grill

Extra-virgin olive oil, for drizzling

Lime wedges, for serving

FOR THE SALSA:

1 ripe but firm mango, peeled and chopped

1 small red onion, thinly sliced

1 bunch cilantro, coarsely chopped

3 tablespoons fresh lime juice

DIRECTIONS

1. Toss mango, onion, cilantro, lime juice, and a big pinch of salt in a medium mixing bowl; drizzle with a bit of olive oil and toss again to coat.
2. Place snapper on a cutting board and pat dry with paper towels. Cut slashes crosswise on a diagonal along the body every 2" on both sides, with a sharp knife, cutting all the way down to the bones.
3. Season fish generously inside and out with salt. Coat fish with tandoori spice.
4. Preheat grill medium-high heat and brush with oil.
5. Grill fish for 10 minutes, undisturbed, until skin is puffed and charred.
6. Flip and grill fish until the other side is lightly charred and skin is puffed, about 8 to 12 minutes.
7. Transfer to a platter.
8. Top with mango salad and serve with lime wedges.

Nutritional Info: Calories: 211, Sodium: 170mg, Dietary Fiber: 2.5g, Fat: 5.4g, Carbs: 18.9g, Protein: 23.6g.

GRILLED OYSTERS WITH SPICED TEQUILA BUTTER

SERVINGS: 6

Prep time: 5 minutes
Cook time: 25 minutes

Tequila infused butter is just the way to elevate oysters fresh off the grill. A delicious appetizer, these oysters are also yummy served with a glass of Sauvignon Blanc or crisp lager and French fries.

INGREDIENTS

3 dozen medium oysters, scrubbed

Flakey sea salt, for serving

FOR THE BUTTER:

1/4 teaspoon crushed red pepper

7 tablespoons unsalted butter

1/4 teaspoon chili oil

1 teaspoon dried oregano

2 tablespoons freshly squeezed lemon juice

2 tablespoons tequila blanco, like Espolon

DIRECTIONS

1. Combine butter ingredients in a small mixing bowl until well-incorporated and set aside.
2. Preheat grill to high.
3. Grill the oysters, flat side up, until they open, about 1 to 2 minutes.
4. Discard the flat top shell and place on a platter; sprinkle with salt flakes.
5. Warm the butter in a microwave for 30 seconds, and spoon the warm tequila butter over the oysters and serve.

Nutritional Info: Calories: 184, Sodium: 300mg, Dietary Fiber: 0.2g, Fat: 15g, Carbs: 3.8g, Protein: 0.2g.

SCALLOPS WITH LEMONY SALSA VERDE

SERVINGS: 2

Prep time: 10 minutes
Cook time: 5 minutes

Brighten up your grilled scallops with a citrus-infused salsa verde. Lemony salsa verde is the perfect compliment to hearty scallops and delicious served alongside risotto or a gorgeous salad.

INGREDIENTS

1 tablespoon olive oil, plus more for grilling

12 large sea scallops, side muscle removed

Sea salt, for seasoning

FOR THE LEMONY SALSA VERDE:

1/2 lemon, with peel, seeded and chopped

5 tomatillos, peeled and pulsed in a blender

1 small shallot, finely chopped

1 garlic clove, finely chopped

1/4 cup olive oil

3/4 cup finely chopped fresh parsley

1/2 cup finely chopped fresh cilantro

1/4 cup chopped fresh chives

1/4 teaspoon sea salt

1/4 teaspoon black pepper

DIRECTIONS

1. Toss Lemony Salsa ingredients in a small mixing bowl and set aside.
2. Preheat grill for medium-high and brush with olive oil.
3. Toss scallops with 1 tablespoon olive oil on a baking sheet and season with salt.
4. Add scallops to grill, turning occasionally, until lightly charred and just cooked through, about 2 minutes per side.
5. Serve scallops topped with Lemony Salsa Verde.

Nutritional Info: Calories: 267, Sodium: 541mg, Dietary Fiber: 3.1g, Fat: 9.6g, Carbs: 13.9g, Protein: 32.4g.

SPICY GRILLED SQUID

SERVINGS: 4

Prep time: 5 minutes
Cook time: 5 minutes

Spice things up with this yummy recipe and serve up some squid at your next dinner party. The perfect appetizer, this is best served on its own or as a decadent appetizer on a bed of leafy greens.

INGREDIENTS

1-1/2 lbs. Squid, prepared
Olive oil

FOR THE MARINADE:

2 cloves garlic cloves, minced
1/2 teaspoon ginger, minced
3 tablespoons gochujang
3 tablespoons corn syrup
1 teaspoon yellow mustard
1 teaspoon soy sauce
2 teaspoons sesame oil
1 teaspoon sesame seeds
2 green onions, chopped

DIRECTIONS

1. Preheat grill to medium high heat and brush with olive oil.
2. Add the squid and tentacles to the grill and cook for 1 minute until the bottom looks firm and opaque.
3. Turn them over and cook for another minute; straighten out the body with tongs if it curls.
4. Baste with sauce on top of the squid and cook 2 additional minutes.
5. Flip and baste the other side, cook 1 minute until the sauce evaporates and the squid turns red and shiny.

Nutritional Info: Calories: 292, Sodium: 466mg, Dietary Fiber: 2.7g, Fat: 8.6g, Carbs: 25.1g, Protein: 27.8g.

SPICED CRAB LEGS

SERVINGS: 4

Prep time: 5 minutes
Cook time: 5 minutes

INGREDIENTS

4 lbs king crab legs, cooked
2 tablespoons chili oil

Crab legs with a twist! If you love spice, you'll love this recipe - but on the chance you just love crab legs you can also substitute chili for olive oil and try it hot and mild!

DIRECTIONS

1. Preheat grill to high.
2. Brush both sides of crab legs with chili oil and place grill.
3. Cook 4 to 5 minutes, turning once.
4. Transfer to plates and serve with drawn butter.

Nutritional Info: Calories: 518, Sodium: 4857mg, Dietary Fiber: 0g, Fat: 13.9g, Carbs: 0g, Protein: 87.1g.

BASTED DUNGENESS CRAB

SERVINGS: 4

Prep time: 5 minutes
Cook time: 5 minutes

Delicate dungeness crab is out of this work when you grill it with a spiced baste. This recipe is sure to capture the heart of any crab lover.

INGREDIENTS

4 lbs dungeness crab legs

FOR THE BASTE:

1/4 cup white wine or white wine vinegar

2 tablespoons sugar

2 tablespoons olive oil

1 tablespoon ginger, minced

1 jalapeno chili, seeded and minced

1 teaspoon, minced garlic

DIRECTIONS

1. Preheat grill to high.
2. Mix baste ingredients together and brush both sides of all crab legs with baste.
3. Cook 4 to 5 minutes, basting often, and turning once.
4. Transfer to plates and serve hot!

Nutritional Info: Calories: 411, Sodium: 1189mg, Dietary Fiber: 3g, Fat: 13.3g, Carbs: 18.4g, Protein: 54.6g.

POP-OPEN CLAMS WITH HORSERADISH-TABASCO SAUCE

SERVINGS: 4

Prep time: 5 minutes
Cook time: 10 minutes

INGREDIENTS

2 dozen littleneck clams, scrubbed

4 tablespoons unsalted butter, softened

2 tablespoons horseradish, drained

1 tablespoon hot sauce, like Tabasco

1/4 teaspoon lemon zest, finely grated

1 tablespoon fresh lemon juice

1/4 teaspoon smoked paprika

Sea salt

These spicy clams are a great way to serve up some decadent seafood right at home. Best served with crusty grilled bread, you'll love this delicious recipe as a starter or side to the perfect dinner.

DIRECTIONS

1. Preheat the grill to high.
2. Blend the butter with the horseradish, hot sauce, lemon zest, lemon juice, paprika, and pinch of salt.
3. Arrange the clams over high heat and grill until they pop open, about 25 seconds.
4. Carefully turn the clams over using tongs, so the meat side is down.
5. Grill for about 20 seconds longer, until the clam juices start to simmer.
6. Transfer the clams to a serving bowl.
7. Top each with about 1/2 teaspoon of the sauce and serve.

Nutritional Info: Calories: 191, Sodium: 382mg, Dietary Fiber: 0.3g, Fat: 12.7g, Carbs: 4g, Protein: 14.8g.

CLAM TOASTS WITH LEMON AND GREEN OLIVES

SERVINGS: 6 - 8

Prep time: 10 minutes
Cook time: 10 minutes

INGREDIENTS

4 lbs. littleneck clams

1 lemon, sliced

1 garlic clove, minced

1/2 cup parsley, coarsely chopped

1 teaspoon crushed red pepper flakes

1/4 cup olive oil, plus more for drizzling

1 loaf crusty bread, halved lengthwise

1 package Green Olive Tapenade

1/3 cup shaved Parmesan

Black Pepper, to taste,

A Mediterranean delicacy, this bruschetta style dish is just to die for! Citrus meats tangy for one delicious way to enjoy clams hot off the grill.

DIRECTIONS

1. Preheat grill to medium-high heat.
2. Grill lemon slices, turning occasionally, until lightly charred, about 2 minutes. Transfer to a cutting board and coarsely chop.
3. Place in a medium mixing bowl and set aside.
4. Add clams to grill. Carefully transfer to a large bowl as they open. (Try to save as much clam liquor as possible).
5. Remove clams from their shells and coarsely chop.
6. Transfer clams and liquor to bowl with lemon and add garlic, parsley, red pepper flakes, and oil; fold gently to combine.
7. Drizzle bread with oil and grill, turning halfway through, until toasted and lightly charred, about 5 minutes.
8. Top toasts with 1 teaspoon Green Olive Tapenade, then clam mixture, sprinkle with Parmesan and serve.

Nutritional Info: Calories: 229, Sodium: 990mg, Dietary Fiber: 1.3g, Fat: 12g, Carbs: 28.9g, Protein: 2.6g.

POTATO SHRIMP FOIL PACKETS

SERVINGS: 4

Prep time: 10 minutes
Cook time: 25 minutes

INGREDIENTS

FOR EACH PACKET:

7 medium sized shrimp, cooked and peeled

3 small red potatoes

1 ear of corn, split in half and shucked clean

2 tablespoons butter

1 tablespoon creole seasoning

You can whip up a shrimp boil style meal for a taste of the Bayou right at home with your gas grill. Just be sure to make plenty for the whole family!

DIRECTIONS

1. Preheat the grill to medium-high.
2. Poke the small red potatoes once or twice with a fork, then place them in the microwave for about 3-5 minutes. Place a long piece of foil on your workstation and fold it in half widthwise.
3. Add the foil packet ingredients, and seal foil to make a packet; repeat until 4 packets are made.
4. Place on grill and cook for about 20 minutes or until heated through and the potatoes are done.
5. Carefully remove from the grill and keep foil wrapped tightly until you are ready to tear open and serve.

Nutritional Info: Calories: 383, Sodium: 1197mg, Dietary Fiber: 3.2g, Fat: 6.4g, Carbs: 29.3g, Protein: 44g.

HONEY-LIME TILAPIA AND CORN FOIL PACK

SERVINGS: 4

Prep time: 10 minutes
Cook time: 10 minutes

INGREDIENTS

4 fillets tilapia

2 tablespoon honey

4 limes, thinly sliced

2 ears corn, shucked

2 tablespoon fresh cilantro leaves

1/4 cup olive oil

Kosher salt

Freshly ground black pepper

The sweet taste of honey and citrus lime come together to infuse flaky tilapia with a flavor sensation out of this world. Serve these yummy foil packs with garden salads and your favorite sparkling beverage.

DIRECTIONS

1. Preheat grill to high.
2. Cut 4 squares of foil about 12" long.
3. Top each piece of foil with a piece of tilapia.
4. Brush tilapia with honey and top with lime, corn and cilantro.
5. Drizzle with olive oil and season with sea salt and pepper.
6. Grill until tilapia is cooked through and corn tender, about 15 minutes.

Nutritional Info: Calories: 319, Sodium: 92mg, Dietary Fiber: 4g, Fat: 14.7g, Carbs: 30.3g, Protein: 24g.

PISTACHIO-LEMON PESTO SHRIMP

SERVINGS: 6

Prep time: 15 minutes
Cook time: 8 minutes

INGREDIENTS

1-1/2 pounds uncooked jumbo shrimp, peeled and deveined

FOR THE PESTO:

1/4 cup basil

1/2 cup fresh parsley, chopped

1/3 cup pistachios, shelled

2 tablespoons lemon juice

1 garlic clove, peeled

1/4 teaspoon lemon zest

1/2 cup olive oil

1/4 cup Parmesan cheese, shaved

1/4 teaspoon salt

1/8 teaspoon pepper

Savory pistachios make for one scrumptious pesto marinade when it comes to grilling shrimp. Serve these shrimp as an appetizer or on a bed of orzo drizzled with olive oil for a lovely meal.

DIRECTIONS

1. Add pesto ingredients to a food processor and process until smooth.
2. Transfer 1/3 cup pesto to a large bowl.
3. Fold in shrimp and toss to coat; refrigerate, covered, 30 minutes.
4. Thread shrimp onto metal skewers.
5. Preheat grill to medium heat.
6. Cook 5-6 minutes, flipping once, until shrimp turn opaque pink.
7. Serve with remaining pesto as a dipping sauce.

Nutritional Info: Calories: 224, Sodium: 1007mg, Dietary Fiber: 0.6g, Fat: 18.7g, Carbs: 1.6g, Protein: 14.8g.

MEXICAN SHRIMP TACOS

SERVINGS: 4

Prep Time: 10 minutes
Cook Time: 10 minutes

Shrimp tacos are a great way to whip up a healthy dinner in no time for the whole family. These tacos are spiced to perfection and will definitely become a family favorite in no time!

INGREDIENTS

2 lbs. Medium shrimp, peeled and deveined

8 flour tortillas, warmed

1 bag cabbage slaw

1 cup salsa

1 cup Mexican crema

FOR MARINADE:

2 tablespoons olive oil

1 tablespoon chili powder

1 tablespoon cumin

1 tablespoon garlic powder

1 tablespoon fresh lime juice

1/4 teaspoon sea salt

1/8 teaspoon fresh ground pepper

DIRECTIONS

1. Preheat a grill to medium-high.
2. Combine oil marinade in a large sealable plastic bag. Add shrimp and toss coat; let marinate in the refrigerator for 30 minutes.
3. Grill shrimp for 3 minutes, on each side, until cooked through.
4. Transfer to a plate.
5. Lay two tortillas on each plate. Evenly divide the shrimp, cabbage slaw, and salsa in the middle of each tortilla.
6. Drizzle with Mexican crema and serve.

Nutritional Info: Calories: 547, Sodium: 1044mg, Dietary Fiber: 5.7g, Fat: 17.4g, Carbs: 37.9g, Protein: 58.8g

FLAKY GRILLED HALIBUT

SERVINGS: 4

Prep time: 5 minutes
Cook time: 10 minutes

Flaky halibut is grilled to perfection in the recipe for the perfect compliment to any salad, bed of brown rice, or grilled vegetables from the recipes below. Just be sure to serve this dish with an oaked Chardonnay to really bring out the flavors.

INGREDIENTS

1 pound fresh halibut filet

FOR THE MARINADE:

2 tablespoons butter, unsalted and melted

2 tablespoons honey

1/2 lemon, juiced

2 teaspoons Worcestershire sauce

1/2 teaspoon black pepper

2 cloves garlic, minced

DIRECTIONS

1. Combine marinade ingredients in a small mixing bowl.
2. Cut halibut filet into 4 (6 ounce) pieces.
3. Brush both sides of each with the marinade.
4. Preheat grill to high.
5. Sear the halibut for 90 seconds on each side.
6. Reduce the heat to medium and cook each side for an additional 2-3 minutes, or until the fish can be easily flaked with a fork.

Nutritional Info: Calories: 250, Sodium: 149mg, Dietary Fiber: 0.3g, Fat: 8.5g, Carbs: 10.5g, Protein: 31g.

SPICY GRILLED JUMBO SHRIMP

SERVINGS: 6

Prep time: 15 minutes
Cook time: 8 minutes

INGREDIENTS

1-1/2 pounds uncooked jumbo shrimp, peeled and deveined

FOR THE MARINADE:

2 tablespoons fresh parsley
1 bay leaf, dried
1 teaspoon chili powder
1 teaspoon garlic powder
1/4 teaspoon cayenne pepper
1/4 cup olive oil
1/4 teaspoon salt
1/8 teaspoon pepper

Spicy grilled shrimp is just out of this world! Top your favorite salads, yellow rice and vegetables, or even serve it on its own for grilling fun.

DIRECTIONS

1. Add marinade ingredients to a food processor and process until smooth.
2. Transfer marinade to a large mixing bowl.
3. Fold in shrimp and toss to coat; refrigerate, covered, 30 minutes.
4. Thread shrimp onto metal skewers.
5. Preheat grill to medium heat.
6. Cook 5-6 minutes, flipping once, until shrimp turn opaque pink.
7. Serve immediately.

Nutritional Info: Calories: 131, Sodium: 980mg, Dietary Fiber: 0.4g, Fat: 8.5g, Carbs: 1g, Protein: 13.7g.

LOBSTER TAILS WITH LIME BASIL BUTTER

SERVINGS: 4

Prep time: 5 minutes
Cook time: 6 minutes

INGREDIENTS

4 lobster tails (cut in half lengthwise)
3 tablespoons olive oil
Lime wedges (to serve)
Sea salt, to taste

FOR THE LIME BASIL BUTTER:

1 stick unsalted butter, softened
1/2 bunch basil, roughly chopped
1 lime, zested and juiced
2 cloves garlic, minced
1/4 teaspoon red pepper flakes

For one amazing dinner, fire up your gas grill and you can grill up lobster tails in less than 10 minutes. Serve them with grilled vegetables, crab legs, and shrimp for a seafood feast.

DIRECTIONS

1. Add the butter ingredients to a mixing bowl and combine; set aside until ready to use.
2. Preheat grill to medium-high heat.
3. Drizzle the lobster tail halves with olive oil and season with salt and pepper.
4. Place the lobster tails, flesh-side down, on the grill.
5. Allow to cook until opaque, about 3 minutes, flip and cook another 3 minutes.
6. Add a dollop of the lime basil butter during the last minute of cooking.
7. Serve immediately.

Nutritional Info: Calories: 430, Sodium: 926mg, Dietary Fiber: 0.5g, Fat: 34.7g, Carbs: 2.4g, Protein: 28g.

COCONUT PINEAPPLE SHRIMP SKEWERS

SERVINGS: 4

Prep time: 1 hour 20 minutes
Cook time: 5 minutes

INGREDIENTS

1-1/2 pounds uncooked jumbo shrimp, peeled and deveined

1/2 cup light coconut milk

1 tablespoon cilantro, chopped

4 teaspoons Tabasco Original Red Sauce

2 teaspoons soy sauce

1/4 cup freshly squeezed orange juice

1/4 cup freshly squeezed lime juice (from about 2 large limes)

3/4 pound pineapple, cut into 1 inch chunks

Olive oil, for grilling

Creamy coconut and fresh pineapple come together to create a taste of Thailand. Serve this decadent shrimp on top a bed of mango sticky rice for one delicious meal.

DIRECTIONS

1. Combine the coconut milk, cilantro, Tabasco sauce, soy sauce, orange juice, and lime juice. Add the shrimp and toss to coat.
2. Cover and place in the refrigerator to marinate for 1 hour.
3. Thread shrimp and pineapple onto metal skewers, alternating each.
4. Preheat grill to medium heat.
5. Cook 5-6 minutes, flipping once, until shrimp turn opaque pink.
6. Serve immediately.

Nutritional Info: Calories: 150, Sodium: 190mg, Dietary Fiber: 1.9g, Fat: 10.8g, Carbs: 14.9g, Protein: 1.5g.

SALMON FILLETS WITH BASIL BUTTER & BROCCOLINI

SERVINGS: 2

Prep time: 10 minutes
Cook time: 12 minutes

INGREDIENTS

2 (6 ounce) salmon fillets, skin removed

2 tablespoons butter, unsalted

2 basil leaves, minced

1 garlic clove, minced

6 ounces broccolini

2 teaspoons olive oil

Sea salt, to taste

Basil infused broccoli is the perfect way to elevate grilled salmon. Healthy and delicious, this recipe is also easy to make on those busy weeknights when you still want to be decadent with dinner.

DIRECTIONS

1. Blend butter, basil, and garlic together until well-incorporated. Form into a ball and place in refrigerator until ready to serve.
2. Preheat grill to medium-high heat.
3. Season both sides of the salmon filets with salt and set aside.
4. Add broccolini, a pinch of salt, and olive oil to a bowl, toss to coat, and set aside.
5. Brush grill with olive oil, and grill salmon for 6 minutes per side for medium.
6. Add the broccoli to the grill, turning occasionally, until slightly charred and golden; about 10-12 minutes.
7. Top each salmon filet topped with a slice of basil butter and serve with a side of broccolini.

Nutritional Info: Calories: 398, Sodium: 303mg, Dietary Fiber: 2.2g, Fat: 26.7g, Carbs: 6.2g, Protein: 35.6g

HALIBUT FILLETS WITH SPINACH AND OLIVES

SERVINGS: 4

Prep time: 10 minutes
Cook time: 10 minutes

INGREDIENTS

4 (6 ounce) halibut fillets

1/3 cup olive oil

4 cups baby spinach

1/4 cup lemon juice

2 ounces pitted black olives, halved

2 tablespoons flat leaf parsley, chopped

2 teaspoons fresh dill, chopped

Lemon wedges, to serve

Fresh flaky fish is perfect served with salty olives and fresh spinach. This recipe makes for one quick and easy dinner any day of the week!

DIRECTIONS

1. Preheat grill to medium heat.
2. Toss spinach with lemon juice in a mixing bowl and set aside.
3. Brush fish with olive oil and cook for 3-4 minutes per side, or until cooked through.
4. Remove from heat, cover with foil and let rest for 5 minutes.
5. Add remaining oil and cook spinach for 2 minutes, or until just wilted. Remove from heat.
6. Toss with olives and herbs, then transfer to serving plates with fish, and serve with lemon wedges.

Nutritional Info: Calories: 773, Sodium: 1112mg, Dietary Fiber: 1.4g, Fat: 36.6g, Carbs: 2.9g, Protein: 109.3g.

SWEET-AND-SMOKY CEDAR-PLANKED SALMON

SERVINGS: 2

Prep time: 2 hours 5 minutes
Cook time: 30 minutes

INGREDIENTS

2 (6 ounce) salmon fillets, skin on

2 tablespoons light brown sugar

2 teaspoon smoked paprika

1 teaspoon lemon zest

1/2 teaspoon sea salt

1/2 teaspoon black pepper

If you're tired of the same-old grilled salmon (don't get me wrong, plain salmon is delicious!), then you can't go wrong with this surprisingly mouthwatering recipe. The smoked paprika, sugar and lemon zest combine to send your taste buds into a state of unexpected bliss.

DIRECTIONS

1. Soak a large cedar grilling plank, in water, for 1 to 2 hours.
2. Heat grill to medium.
3. Combine sugar, paprika, lemon zest, salt and pepper in a bowl; season salmon on flesh side.
4. Place salmon on soaked plank, skin side down. Grill, tented with foil, for 25 to 28 minutes for medium.
5. Serve immediately with your favorite sides.

Nutritional Info: Calories: 267, Sodium: 547mg, Dietary Fiber: 1g, Fat: 10.8.g, Carbs:10.6g, Protein: 33.4g.

CHAPTER 8
BURGERS

JUICY LUCY BURGER

SERVINGS: 2

Prep time: 10 minutes
Cook time: 10 minutes

INGREDIENTS

1 lb. ground chuck

4 slices yellow American cheese

1 tomato, sliced

1 head iceberg lettuce chopped

2 hamburger buns

Salt and black pepper

This classic stuffed burger takes the classic American burger and injects the cheese right into the patty for a delicious and fun night of grilling!

DIRECTIONS

1. Form the ground chuck into four thin burger patties, and season with salt and pepper.
2. Place two slices of cheese in the middle of two of the patties. Then place the other patties on top of the cheese and form the meat around the cheese so that no cheese is visible.
3. Light your grill and turn to medium-high heat.
4. When the grill is hot, place the burgers on the grill, and cook for approximately three minutes, then flip and keep cooking an additional three minutes..
5. When burgers are finished cooking, remove from the grill and allow to rest on a plate for five minutes. While the burgers rest, toast the buns on the grill.
6. Place the burgers on the buns and top with lettuce and tomatoes.

Nutritional Info: Calories: 138, Sodium: 315mg, Dietary Fiber: 1.3g, Fat: 10.6.g, Carbs: 7.8g, Protein: 5.7g.

BREAKFAST BURGER

SERVINGS: 4

Prep time: 10 minutes
Cook time: 10 minutes

INGREDIENTS

1 lb. ground sausage

4 large eggs, fried over easy

4 brioche buns

2 tablespoons butter

4 slices cheddar or American cheese

Hot sauce (optional)

A gas grill is also perfect for breakfast and this hearty breakfast burger is sure to please the whole family.

DIRECTIONS

1. Form the sausage into four patties and set aside.
2. Light your grill and set to medium-high heat.
3. Place the sausage patties on the grill and cook 4 minutes per side or until cooked through.
4. Spread the butter evenly on the buns and place, butter side down, on the grill. Cook until just browned. Remove from the grill.
5. Place the cheese on the sausage patties and cook until it melts.
6. Remove the sausage patties from the grill and place on the buns.
7. Add the fried eggs and a dash of hot sauce, and serve immediately.

Nutritional Info: Calories: 173, Sodium: 243mg, Dietary Fiber: 4.2g, Fat: 13.2g, Carbs: 16.1g, Protein: 2.7g.

BLACK FOREST BURGER

SERVINGS: 4

Prep Time: 15 minutes
Cook Time: 10 minutes

INGREDIENTS

2 lbs. ground chuck

4 slices Black Forest ham

8 slices brie cheese

3 tablespoons Dijon mustard

4 brioche buns

2 tablespoons butter

Salt and black pepper

A fun way to incorporate French flavors into the classic American burger, this Black Forest burger is easy to make, and sure to be a hit..

DIRECTIONS

1. Preheat grill to medium-high, and form the chuck into four equal patties. Season the patties with salt and pepper.
2. Place burgers on the grill and cook until desired doneness is reached.
3. Add brie to the burgers and cook until cheese has melted, then remove burgers from the grill and allow to rest for five minutes.
4. While burgers rest, spread the butter on the buns and toast until browned. Remove from the grill and spread the mustard evenly on the buns.
5. Place the burgers on the buns and top each burger with a slice of Black Forest ham before serving.

Nutritional Info: Calories: 132, Sodium: 246mg, Dietary Fiber: 1.3g, Fat: 8.9g, Carbs: 13.7g, Protein: 1.9g.

PIZZA BURGER

SERVINGS: 4

Prep time: 10 minutes
Cook time: 15 minutes

INGREDIENTS

2 lbs. ground chuck

4 slices low-moisture mozzarella cheese

1 cup marinara sauce

16 slices pepperoni

1 teaspoon dried oregano

4 kaiser rolls

Salt and black pepper

Can't decide between pizza and burgers tonight? Worry not, this burger combines the best of both, and it's super easy to make.

DIRECTIONS

1. Preheat the grill to medium-high heat. Form the chuck into four equal patties and season with salt and pepper.
2. Place patties on the grill and cook for four minutes. Flip the burgers and place four slices of pepperoni on each patty, then top each patty with a slice of cheese.
3. Grill the burgers until they have achieved desired doneness and remove from the grill.
4. Place the burgers on the rolls and top with a spoonful of marinara sauce. Sprinkle on a pinch of oregano and serve.

Nutritional Info: Calories: 298, Sodium: 751mg, Dietary Fiber: 5.8g, Fat: 20.1g, Carbs: 28.9g, Protein: 6.2g.

TEXAS CHILI BURGER

SERVINGS: 4

Prep time: 10 minutes
Cook time: 15 minutes

INGREDIENTS

2 lbs. ground chuck

1 cups Texas-style chili

4 Potato buns

4 oz. sharp cheddar cheese, grated

2 tablespoons butter

Salt and black pepper

Hot sauce (optional)

Whether or not you like beans in your chili, everyone can agree that chili and burgers go perfectly with each other. This Texas-style burger is quick and easy to make.

DIRECTIONS

1. Preheat grill to medium-high heat. Form the chuck into four equal size patties. Season with salt and pepper

2. Spread the butter on the buns and place butter side down on the grill. Toast until golden brown.

3. Place burgers on the grill and cook for four minutes. Flip and top with the grated cheese. Cook an additional four to five minutes.

4. Remove the burgers from the grill and transfer to the buns. Top each burger with a scoop of chili and serve with hot sauce.

Nutritional Info: Calories: 73, Sodium: 314mg, Dietary Fiber: 0.9g, Fat: 7.1g, Carbs: 3.1g, Protein: 0.5g.

BALSAMIC PORTOBELLO BURGER

SERVINGS: 2

Prep time: 10 minutes
Cook time: 15 minutes

Looking for a vegetarian alternative to your traditional burger? Look no further. This grilled portobello burger is perfect for those times when you want a lighter meal, but you don't want to sacrifice flavour.

INGREDIENTS

- 2 Portobello mushrooms
- 4 tablespoons balsamic vinegar
- 2 tablespoons olive oil
- 2 slices Swiss cheese
- 1 cup spring mix
- Salt and black pepper.
- 2 Brioche buns

DIRECTIONS

1. Preheat the grill to medium-high heat. Brush the portobellos with a little of the vinegar and season with salt and pepper.
2. In a bowl, combine the oil and two tablespoons of balsamic vinegar, and add the spring mix. Mix until coated.
3. Place the portobellos on the grill and cook until softened and a little charred. Place the cheese on the portobellos and remove from the grill.
4. Place the portobellos on the buns and top with the spring mix.

Nutritional Info: Calories: 283, Sodium: 866mg, Dietary Fiber: 0.6g, Fat: 25.1.g, Carbs: 2.9g, Protein: 12.7g.

SPICED TURKEY BURGER

SERVINGS: 4

Prep time: 15 minutes
Cook time: 15 minutes

INGREDIENTS

1-1/2 lb. ground turkey
4 potato buns
1 red onion, sliced
4 slices sharp cheddar cheese
1 teaspoon smoked paprika
1 teaspoon garlic powder
1 teaspoon onion powder
1/2 teaspoon curry powder
2 teaspoons salt
1/2 teaspoon black pepper

Turkey is a great substitute for traditional beef burgers and these burgers add savory flavors to be the best turkey burger you've ever had.

DIRECTIONS

1. Preheat a grill to medium-high heat.
2. Form the ground turkey into four equal patties and set aside.
3. In a small bowl, combine the paprika, garlic powder, onion powder, curry powder, salt, and pepper. Mix well.
4. Season the turkey patties with the spice mix and place on grill. Cook for five minutes, and flip. Add the cheese and cook until melted, about five minutes.
5. Remove the burgers from the grill and place on the buns with sliced red onion.

Nutritional Info: Calories: 521, Sodium: 521mg, Dietary Fiber: 7.7g, Fat: 22.3.g, Carbs: 72.1g, Protein: 12g.

SALMON BURGERS

SERVINGS: 4

Prep time: 20 minutes
Cook time: 30 minutes

INGREDIENTS

1-1/2 lb. Salmon filets, skin removed and chopped

1/2 red onion, finely chopped

1/4 cup dill, finely chopped

2 tablespoons mayonnaise

1/4 cup breadcrumbs

2 tablespoons Dijon mustard

4 brioche buns

2 tablespoons butter

Salt and black pepper

Lighter than your traditional burger, but bursting with flavour, these salmon burgers are perfect for grilling on a hot summer night.

DIRECTIONS

1. In a large bowl, combine the salmon, onion, dill, mayo, breadcrumbs, mustard, salt and pepper. Mix until combined.
2. Heat your grill to medium heat.
3. Spread the butter on the buns, and toast on the grill until golden brown.
4. Form the salmon mixture into four equal patties. Place on the grill and cook for ten minutes. Flip and continue cooking until cooked through.
5. Remove the burgers from the grill and set aside to rest for five minutes.
6. Place the burgers on the buns and serve.

Nutritional Info: Calories: 328, Sodium: 492mg, Dietary Fiber: 7.4g, Fat: 24.7.g, Carbs: 27.7g, Protein: 4.9g.

CALIFORNIA BURGER

SERVINGS: 4

Prep time: 10 minutes
Cook time: 15 minutes

INGREDIENTS

2 lbs. ground chuck
1 avocado, sliced
8 slices bacon
4 slices American cheese
3 tablespoons cilantro, chopped
4 burger buns
2 tablespoons mayonnaise
Salt and black pepper

The classic American burger with a twist. This burger is fun and a little bit healthier, but still packed with flavour.

DIRECTIONS

1. Set your grill to medium-high heat and form the chuck into four equal patties. Season the patties with salt and pepper.
2. Place the patties on the grill and cook for five minutes. Flip, add the cheese and cook an additional 5 minutes.
3. Toast the buns until golden brown and remove from grill.
4. Spread the mayo on the bottoms of the buns. Place the burgers on the buns and add the bacon, avocado, and a sprinkle of cilantro.

Nutritional Info: Calories: 343, Sodium: 606mg, Dietary Fiber: 7.1g, Fat: 17.3g, Carbs: 44.9g, Protein: 5g.

SAUTEED MUSHROOM BURGER

SERVINGS: 4

Prep time: 15 minutes
Cook time: 20 minutes

INGREDIENTS

2 lbs. ground chuck

1 lb. white or button mushrooms, sliced

½ yellow onion, finely chopped

1/4 cup canola oil

1/4 cup balsamic vinegar

4 slices Swiss cheese

4 Onion buns

Salt and black pepper

Savory and a little sweet, this burger packs complex flavor for a fun way to shake up your typical burger night.

DIRECTIONS

1. Preheat grill to medium-high heat and heat a saucepan over medium heat.
2. To the saucepan, add the oil and onions. Cook until transparent, and then add the mushrooms. Cook until the mushrooms are soft, then add the vinegar. Cook until vinegar has reduced into a thick sauce. Remove from heat.
3. Season the burgers and place them on the grill. Cook for five minutes, flip and add the cheese. Continue to cook for an additional four to five minutes.
4. Remove the burgers from the grill and place on the buns. Add a generous scoop of the mushroom mix to the burgers and serve.

BLT BURGER

SERVINGS: 4

Prep time: 15 minutes
Cook time: 15 minutes

INGREDIENTS

1 lb. Ground chuck
1 head iceberg lettuce, chopped
1 tomato, sliced
8 slices of bacon, cooked
4 slices American cheese
4 burger buns
4 tablespoons mayonnaise
Salt and black pepper

Everyone loves a burger, and everyone loves a BLT. Why not have both at the same time?

DIRECTIONS

1. Set your grill to medium-high heat, and form the chuck into four equal patties. Season with salt and pepper.
2. Place the burgers on the grill and cook for three minutes, flip, and top with cheese. Continue cooking for an additional two to three minutes.
3. Toast the buns on the grill until golden brown. Remove the buns from the grill and spread the mayo on the bottom buns.
4. Remove the burgers from the grill and place on the buns. Top with bacon, lettuce, and tomato to serve.

Nutritional Info: Calories: 210, Sodium: 1564mg, Dietary Fiber: 5.4g, Fat: 15.1g, Carbs: 17.4g, Protein: 7.7g

TACO BURGER

SERVINGS: 4

Prep time: 10 minutes
Cook time: 15 minutes

INGREDIENTS

2 lbs. ground chuck

1 packet taco seasoning

4 slices sharp cheddar cheese

4 potato buns

1 tomato

1 head iceberg lettuce

1 tablespoon hot sauce (optional)

Half taco, half burger, this south of the border treat is the best of both worlds.

DIRECTIONS

1. Preheat your grill to medium-high.
2. In a large bowl, combine the chuck and taco seasoning and mix well to combine. Form the beef into four patties.
3. Place the burgers on the grill and cook for five minutes. Flip and add the cheese to the burgers. Cook an additional five minutes.
4. Transfer the burgers to the buns and top with lettuce, tomato, and hot sauce to serve.

Nutritional Info: Calories: 97, Sodium: 182mg, Dietary Fiber: 4.4g, Fat: 4.3g, Carbs: 12.8g, Protein: 4.5g.

GORGONZOLA LAMB BURGER

SERVINGS: 4

Prep time: 10 minutes
Cook time: 15 minutes

INGREDIENTS

2 lbs. ground lamb

1 cup gorgonzola cheese

4 onion or Kaiser buns

2 tablespoons whole grain mustard

Salt and black pepper

Lamb is rich in flavour as well as very tender. Robust gorgonzola adds a complex flavour, both tangy and earthy.

DIRECTIONS

1. Preheat grill to medium-high.
2. Chop the gorgonzola and set aside.
3. Add the burgers to the grill and cook for five minutes. Flip, add the a scoop of gorgonzola to each burger. Cook for an additional five minutes.
4. Toast the buns and spread the whole grain mustard on the bottom buns.
5. Transfer the burgers to the buns and serve.

Nutritional Info: Calories: 61, Sodium: 158mg, Dietary Fiber: 2.9g, Fat: 4.9g, Carbs: 4.9g, Protein: 0.8g.

EGGPLANT CAPRESE BURGER

SERVINGS: 4

Prep time: 5 minutes
Cook time: 10 minutes

INGREDIENTS

1 eggplant, sliced into 1/2 inch rounds
1 tomato, sliced into rounds
1 ball fresh mozzarella cheese
6 basil leaves, chopped
4 ciabatta buns
2 tablespoons olive oil
2 tablespoons balsamic vinegar
Salt and black pepper.

Another great alternative to a regular burger, this eggplant caprese burger is delicious and vegetarian.

DIRECTIONS

1. Preheat grill to medium heat.
2. Season the eggplant with salt and pepper, and place on the grill. Grill for three to four minutes and flip. Cook another three minutes.
3. Place slices of tomato on the bottom bun and top with mozzarella. When the eggplant is finished cooking. Place on top of the mozzarella.
4. Drizzle the eggplant with olive oil and vinegar, and sprinkle with basil before serving.

Nutritional Info: Calories: 115, Sodium: 407mg, Dietary Fiber: 2.9g, Fat: 8.7g, Carbs: 8.4g, Protein: 3.6g.

BCO BURGER

SERVINGS: 4

Prep time: 10 minutes
Cook time: 10 minutes

INGREDIENTS

2 lbs. ground chuck

4 slices sharp cheddar cheese

1 cup caramelized onions

8 slices thick cut bacon

4 kaiser rolls

2 tablespoons spicy brown mustard

Salt and black pepper

This Bacon Cheese Onion burger is reminiscent of famous (and gloriously delicious) versions found in some popular restaurants. Enjoy with you favorite ice cold soda or beer!

DIRECTIONS

1. Preheat grill to medium-high heat.
2. Form the chuck into four equal patties, and season with salt and pepper.
3. Place on the grill and cook for five minutes. Flip, add the cheese and continue cooking for an additional five minutes.
4. Toast the buns on the grill and spread the mustard on the bottom buns.
5. Place the burgers on the buns and top with bacon and onions.

Nutritional Info: Calories: 94, Sodium: 316mg, Dietary Fiber: 1.2g, Fat: 7.2g, Carbs: 4.7g, Protein: 0.9g.

RUEBEN BURGER

SERVINGS: 4

Prep time: 10 minutes
Cook time: 15 minutes

INGREDIENTS

1 lb. ground chuck

1 cup sauerkraut

4 tablespoons Russian dressing

4 slices Swiss cheese

1 lb. pastrami

4 onion buns

Salt and black pepper

A perfect combination of the classic Rueben sandwich and a classic burger.

DIRECTIONS

1. Preheat grill to medium-high heat.
2. Form the chuck into four equal patties. Season with salt and pepper, and place on the grill.
3. Cook burgers for three minutes, flip, and add the Swiss cheese.
4. Spread the Russian dressing on the buns, and place an equal amount of pastrami on each bottom bun.
5. Place the burgers on the pastrami and top with sauerkraut.

Nutritional Info: Calories: 102, Sodium: 171mg, Dietary Fiber: 1.6g, Fat: 7.8g, Carbs: 3.8g, Protein: 6.2g.

CHAPTER 9
SANDWICHES & BREADS

CHEESY HAM AND PINEAPPLE SANDWICH

SERVINGS: 4

Prep time: 10 minutes
Cook time: 20 minutes

INGREDIENTS

1 (10 ounce) package deli sliced ham, like Sam's Choice Uncured Honey Ham

4 pineapple rings

4 slices swiss cheese

4 buns, like potato or brioche

Butter, softened, for brushing

Poppy seeds, for brushing

Ooey, gooey cheese meets sweet pineapple and ham for one delicious sandwich. Fix these up for a lunch time treat or double the recipe for a family get together for easy fun food to serve on the weekends.

DIRECTIONS

1. Cut a large piece of aluminum foil into four squares, large enough to wrap sandwiches in, and place on a flat work surface.
2. On top of each foil piece, stack a bottom bun, 1/4 of the ham, a pineapple ring, and 1 slice of cheese.
3. Place the top bun on top and brush with melted butter; when all sandwiches are built sprinkle poppy seeds on top.
4. Wrap the sandwiches with foil and leave the top slightly loose.
5. Preheat to medium-high and grill for 20 minutes.
6. Let cool slightly, unwrap, and enjoy!

Nutritional Info: Calories: 594, Sodium: 3184mg, Dietary Fiber: 0.3g, Fat: 40.3g, Carbs: 4.7g, Protein: 47.7g.

GARLIC PARMESAN GRILLED CHEESE SANDWICHES

SERVINGS: 1

Prep time: 2 minutes
Cook time: 7 minutes

INGREDIENTS

2 slices Italian bread, sliced thin

2 slices provolone cheese

2 tablespoons butter, softened

Garlic powder, for dusting

Dried parsley, for dusting

Parmesan Cheese, shredded, for dusting

Give your grilled cheese a gourmet twist when you elevate them with tangy parmesan cheese. This is my favorite way to enjoy a big bowl of tomato soup or grilled salad in the recipes above.

DIRECTIONS

1. Spread butter evenly across 2 slices of bread and sprinkle each buttered side with garlic and parsley.
2. Sprinkle a few tablespoons of Parmesan cheese over each buttered side of bread and gently press the cheese into the bread.
3. Preheat the grill to medium heat and place one slice of bread, buttered side down into the skillet.
4. Top with provolone slices and second slice of bread with the butter side up.
5. Cook, 3 minutes and flip to cook 3 minutes on the other side; cook until bread is golden and parmesan cheese is crispy.
6. Serve warm with your favorite sides!

Nutritional Info: Calories: 575, Sodium: 1065mg, Dietary Fiber: 2.8g, Fat: 45.1g, Carbs: 18.1g, Protein: 27.6g.

GRILLED VEGGIE PANINI

SERVINGS: 4

Prep time: 12 minutes
Cook time: 20 minutes

Hearty and robust, this panini is stuffed with delicious vegetables that really pack a punch. You'll love this hearty sandwich served with carrot sticks and hummus or a bag of kettle chips, and sparkling lemonade or kombucha.

INGREDIENTS

8 slices sourdough bread

1 small zucchini, cut into strips

1 small yellow squash, cut into strips

1 red bell pepper, cut into strips

1 small red onion, cut into strips

3 basil leaves, chopped

2 teaspoons olive oil

Sea salt, to taste

Pepper, to taste

8 slices provolone cheese

2 tablespoons mayonnaise

DIRECTIONS

1. Preheat entire grill for medium heat.
2. Toss vegetables, olive oil, basil, salt and pepper in a large mixing bowl.
3. Add to the grill and cook 5 minutes flipping often, until vegetables are softened.
4. Remove from the grill. Top 4 bread slices with mayonnaise, grilled veggies, cheese, and second slice of bread.
5. Place on the grill and cook for about 3 minutes per side.
6. Remove and serve warm.

Nutritional Info: Calories: 452, Sodium: 1022mg, Dietary Fiber: 2.7g, Fat: 21g, Carbs: 44g, Protein: 22.8g.

GRILLED PIZZA CHEESE

SERVINGS: 4

Prep Time: 10 minutes
Cook Time: 20 minutes

INGREDIENTS

8 slices French bread

3 tablespoons butter, softened

1/2 cup pizza sauce

1/4 cup mozzarella cheese

1/2 cup pepperoni diced

Garlic powder, for dusting

Oregano, for dusting

Pizza lovers rejoice! You can whip up quick and easy Pizza Grilled Cheese on your gas grill for the whole family in no time.

DIRECTIONS

1. Spread butter on one side of each French bread slice.
2. Place butter side down on a piece of aluminum foil and dust with garlic powder and oregano.
3. Spread pizza sauce on opposite side of all French bread slices.
4. Top 4 slices of bread with mozzarella cheese, a few slices of pepperoni, and additional mozzarella.
5. Place remaining French bread slices on top of pizza topped bread, butter side up, to create 4 sandwiches.
6. Preheat the grill to medium heat and place one slice of bread, buttered side down into the skillet.
7. Cook, 3 minutes and flip to cook 3 minutes on the other side; cook until bread is golden and cheese is melted.
8. Serve warm and enjoy!

Nutritional Info: Calories: 305, Sodium: 664mg, Dietary Fiber: 2.3g, Fat: 12g, Carbs: 40.4g, Protein: 9.4g.

TURKEY PESTO PANINI

SERVINGS: 2

Prep time: 5 minutes
Cook time: 6 minutes

INGREDIENTS

1 tablespoon olive oil

4 slices French bread

1/2 cup pesto sauce

4 slices mozzarella cheese

2 cups chopped leftover turkey

1 Roma tomatoes, thinly sliced

1 avocado, halved, seeded, peeled and sliced

Turkey Pesto Paninis are the perfect quick sandwich to whip up when you are pressed for time. This recipe is delicious served with any soup or salad for one hearty weekday meal or something fun on the weekends.

DIRECTIONS

1. Preheat grill to medium-high heat.
2. Brush each slice of bread with olive oil on one side.
3. Place 2 slices olive oil side down on aluminum foil.
4. Spread 2 tablespoons pesto over 1 side of French bread.
5. Top with one slice mozzarella, turkey, tomatoes, avocado, a second slice of mozzarella, and top with second half of bread to make a sandwich; repeat with remaining slices of bread.
6. Grill until the bread is golden and the cheese is melted, about 2-3 minutes per side.
7. Serve warm with your favorite salad or soup.

Nutritional Info: Calories: 1129, Sodium: 1243mg, Dietary Fiber: 10g, Fat: 70.9g, Carbs: 53.2g, Protein: 73g.

GREEK CHICKEN SALAD PITA POCKETS

SERVINGS: 6

Prep time: 10 minutes
Cook time: 5 minutes

INGREDIENTS

6 whole wheat pita pockets, halved

FOR THE SANDWICH STUFFING:

1 cup leftover grilled chicken thighs, chopped

4 cups shredded romaine lettuce

1/4 cup chopped grape tomatoes

1/2 cup chopped cucumber

1/4 cup black olives, sliced

1/3 cup crumbled feta

FOR THE GREEK DRESSING:

1/4 cup extra-virgin olive oil

2 tablespoons red wine vinegar

1 lemon, juiced

2 cloves garlic, minced

1 teaspoon dried oregano

Sea salt, to taste

Pepper, to taste

When you need a recipe for leftover grilled chicken, this is the way to go! Otherwise, this recipe is delicious for those who love to meal prep. Just follow a recipe above for your favorite grilled chicken and you can whip these up in no time.

DIRECTIONS

1. Whisk together dressing ingredients in a large mixing bowl. Add the sandwich stuffing ingredients to bowl and toss in dressing until well-coated.
2. Fill each pita pocket with Chicken Salad and enjoy!

Nutritional Info: Calories: 252, Sodium: 264mg, Dietary Fiber: 4g, Fat: 13.2g, Carbs: 23.8g, Protein: 13.5g.

MINI PORTOBELLO BURGERS

SERVINGS: 4

Prep time: 15 minutes
Cook time: 15 minutes

INGREDIENTS

4 portobello mushroom caps
4 slices mozzarella cheese
4 buns, like brioche

FOR THE MARINADE:

1/4 cup balsamic vinegar
2 tablespoons olive oil
1 teaspoon dried basil
1 teaspoon dried oregano
1 teaspoon garlic powder
1/4 teaspoon sea salt
1/4 teaspoon black pepper

Delicious and nutritious, these Mini Portobello Burgers are a great animal protein alternative and wonderful for those wanting to add veggies to their healthy lifestyle. Simple and easy, serve them with a side of turnip fries or sweet potato friends for a low-calorie meal.

DIRECTIONS

1. Whisk together marinade ingredients in a large mixing bowl. Add mushroom caps and toss to coat.
2. Let stand at room temperature for 15 minutes, turning twice.
3. Preheat grill for medium-high heat.
4. Place mushrooms on the grill; reserve marinade for basting.
5. Grill for 5 to 8 minutes on each side, or until tender.
6. Brush with marinade frequently.
7. Top with mozzarella cheese during the last 2 minutes of grilling.
8. Remove from grill and serve on brioche buns.

Nutritional Info: Calories: 248, Sodium: 429mg, Dietary Fiber: 2.1g, Fat: 13.5g, Carbs: 20.3g, Protein: 13g.

LAYERED BEEF & CORN BURGER

SERVINGS: 6

Prep time: 20 minutes
Cook time: 30 minutes

INGREDIENTS

1 large egg, lightly beaten

1 cup whole kernel corn, cooked

1/2 cup bread crumbs

2 tablespoons shallots, minced

1 teaspoon Worcestershire sauce

2 pounds ground beef

1 teaspoon salt

1/2 teaspoon pepper

1/2 teaspoon ground sage

Whip up something different for dinner with this hearty Corn Burger!

DIRECTIONS

1. Combine the egg, corn, bread crumbs, shallots, and Worcestershire sauce in a mixing bowl and set aside.
2. Combine ground beef and seasonings in a separate bowl.
3. Line a flat surface with waxed paper.
4. Roll beef mixture into 12 thin burger patties.
5. Spoon corn mixture into the center of 6 patties and spread evenly across within an inch of the edge
6. Top each with a second circle of meat and press edges to seal corn mixture in the middle of each burger.
7. Grill over medium heat, for 12-15 minutes on each side or until thermometer reads 160°F and juices run clear.

Nutritional Info: Calories: 354, Sodium: 578mg, Dietary Fiber: 1.2g Fat: 11.1g, Carbs: 12.3g, Protein: 49.1g.

PROSCIUTTO PESTO HOT DOG

SERVINGS: 4

Prep time: 15 minutes
Cook time: 15 minutes

INGREDIENTS

4 smoked turkey hot dogs,
like Oscar Meyer Uncured Turkey Dogs

4 large hot dog buns or split top hoagies

6 ounces fresh mozzarella cheese

1/3 cup pesto, divided

3 ounces prosciutto, sliced thinly

1/4 cup marinate artichoke
hearts, chopped

Olive oil, for drizzling

Parmesan cheese, shaved for garnish.

These gourmet hot dogs will knock the socks off of any guest you serve them to! Just be sure to pair it with gourmet kettle chips, a grilled salad from the recipes below, and an ice cold craft beer or your favorite soft drink.

DIRECTIONS

1. Preheat the entire grill to medium heat.
2. Add hot dogs, to one side, and reduce that side's heat to low. Grill until cooked through; about 5 to 7 minutes; turning occasionally.
3. Fry the sliced prosciutto until crispy on the other side of the grill; about 3 minutes. Drain on a paper towel lined plate; and set aside.
4. In the last minute on the grill, top the hot dogs with thin slices of the mozzarella cheese, and remove once the cheese is melted.
5. Toast the buns on the grill for 2 minutes and remove.
6. Spread pesto onto the toasted buns.
7. Top with mozzarella covered hot dog.
8. Top with crispy prosciutto, artichoke hearts, parmesan cheese and a drizzle of olive oil.
9. Serve immediately!

Nutritional Info: Calories: 457, Sodium: 1166mg, Dietary Fiber: 1.5g, Fat: 25.8g, Carbs: 26.3g, Protein: 29.9g.

CURRY PORK WRAPS WITH NECTARINE CHUTNEY

SERVINGS: 3 - 6

Prep time: 2 hours 10 minutes
Cook time: 25 minutes

INGREDIENTS

1 (3/4 lb.) pork tenderloin
6 wheat tortillas
Cucumber slices, for serving
Red onion slices, for serving
Baby spinach, for serving

FOR THE MARINADE:

1 cup Greek yogurt, plain
3 tablespoon lime juice
2 tablespoon mild yellow curry powder
1 teaspoon cumin
1/2 teaspoon pepper
1/2 teaspoon salt
1/4 teaspoon ground nutmeg

FOR THE NECTARINE CHUTNEY:

2 cups nectarines, chopped
1/3 cup mango chutney
2 tablespoon apple cider vinegar
2 tablespoon fresh cilantro, chopped
2 tablespoon fresh mint, chopped
1/2 teaspoon salt
1/2 teaspoon pepper

Curried pork is a delicious way to enjoy your gas grill - especially when you use it to stuff luscious wraps for one delicious way to enjoy lunch or dinner.

DIRECTIONS

1. Combine marinade ingredients in a large mixing bowl.
2. Cut 4 (1-inch) slits into the pork tenderloin. Add pork to marinade, turning to coat, cover and marinate in the refrigerator for 2 to 24 hours.
3. Combine chutney ingredients in a bowl; cover and refrigerate until ready to assemble wraps.
4. Remove pork from marinade.
5. Preheat grill to medium-high heat, and cook 10 to 12 minutes on each side or until a meat thermometer inserted into thickest portion registers 155°F.
6. Remove from grill and let stand 10 minutes.
7. Slice pork thin. Layer a tortilla with slices of pork, baby spinach, cucumber slices, red onion and a dollop of nectarine chutney.
8. Serve immediately and enjoy.

Nutritional Info: Calories: 248, Sodium: 516mg, Dietary Fiber: 10g Fat: 5.3g, Carbs: 28.6g, Protein: 22.4g.

SUN-DRIED TOMATO AND CHICKEN FLATBREADS

SERVINGS: 4

Prep time: 5 minutes
Cook time: 7 minutes

INGREDIENTS

4 flat breads or thin pita bread

FOR THE TOPPING:

1-1/2 cups of sliced grilled chicken, pre-cooked or leftovers

1/2 cup sun-dried tomatoes, coarsely chopped

6 leaves fresh basil, coarsely chopped

3 cups mozzarella cheese, shredded

1 teaspoon salt

1 teaspoon ground black pepper

1 teaspoon red pepper flakes

Olive or chili oil, for serving

Grilled chicken flatbreads are a perfect afternoon snack or lunch option. Serve with a salad for a full meal or enjoy on its own with friends and family on a sunny afternoon with sparkling water.

DIRECTIONS

1. Preheat the grill to low heat.
2. Mix all the topping ingredients together in a large mixing bowl with a rubber spatula.
3. Lay flatbreads on grill, and top with an even amount of topping mixture; spreading to the edges of each.
4. Tent the flatbreads with foil for 5 minutes each, or until cheese is just melted.
5. Place flatbreads on a flat surface or cutting board, and cut each with a pizza cutter or kitchen scissors.
6. Drizzle with olive or chili oil to serve!

Nutritional Info: Calories: 276, Sodium: 1061mg, Dietary Fiber: 1.9g, Fat: 5.7g, Carbs: 35.7g, Protein: 19.8g.

BACON JALAPENO WRAPS

SERVINGS: 4

Prep time: 5 minutes
Cook time: 10 minutes

INGREDIENTS

1 package bacon,
uncured and nitrate free

6 fresh jalapeno peppers,
halved lengthwise and seeded

1 (8 ounce) package cream cheese

When bacon meets jalapeno you have a flavor explosion from out of this world! Serve these delicious spicy wraps at your next family get together or tailgate party with cool veggies like carrot and celery sticks on the side.

DIRECTIONS

1. Preheat an outdoor grill for high heat.
2. Fill jalapeno halves with cream cheese.
3. Wrap each with bacon. Secure with a toothpick.
4. Place on the grill, and cook until bacon is crispy, about 5 to 7 minutes per side.
5. Remove to a platter to cool and serve warm.

Nutritional Info: Calories: 379, Sodium: 1453mg, Dietary Fiber: 0.9g, Fat: 33.4g, Carbs: 3.5g, Protein: 16.3g.

VEGGIE PESTO FLATBREAD

SERVINGS: 4

Prep time: 40 minutes
Cook time: 10 minutes

INGREDIENTS

2 prepared flatbreads
1 jar pesto
1 cup shredded mozzarella cheese

FOR THE TOPPING:

1/2 cup cherry tomatoes, halved
1 small red onion, sliced thin
1 red bell pepper, sliced
1 yellow bell pepper, sliced
1/2 cup mixed black and green olives, halved
1 small yellow squash or zucchini, sliced
2 teaspoons olive oil
1/4 teaspoon sea salt
1/4 teaspoon black pepper

Grilled Veggie Pesto Flatbreads are simply perfect for any weekend or party with family and friends. When it comes to having Vegetarian options for everyone, this is a great way to create a special sharing flatbread so everyone is included in the grilling fun.

DIRECTIONS

1. Preheat the grill to low heat.
2. Spread an even amount of pesto onto each flatbread.
3. Top with 1/2 cup mozzarella cheese each.
4. Mix all the topping ingredients together in a large mixing bowl with a rubber spatula.
5. Lay flatbreads on grill, and top with an even amount of topping mixture; spreading to the edges of each.
6. Tent the flatbreads with foil for 5 minutes each, or until cheese is just melted.
7. Place flatbreads on a flat surface or cutting board, and cut each with a pizza cutter or kitchen scissors.
8. Serve warm!

Nutritional Info: Calories: 177, Sodium: 482mg, Dietary Fiber: 1.7g, Fat: 11.9g, Carbs: 12.6g, Protein: 5.5g.

GRILLED VEGETABLE PIZZA

SERVINGS: 6

Prep time: 30 minutes
Cook time: 10 minutes

INGREDIENTS

8 small fresh mushrooms, halved

1 small zucchini, cut into 1/4-inch slices

1 small yellow pepper, sliced

1 small red pepper, sliced

1 small red onion, sliced

1 tablespoon white wine vinegar

1 tablespoon water

4 teaspoons olive oil, divided

1/2 teaspoon dried basil

1/4 teaspoon sea salt

1/4 teaspoon pepper

1 prebaked 12-inch thin whole wheat pizza crust

1 can (8 ounces) pizza sauce

2 small tomatoes, chopped

2 cups shredded part-skim mozzarella cheese

Grilled Vegetable Pizzas are a great weeknight treat or a way to use the summer vegetables in your garden. Just be sure to get creative with your toppings and really savor this delicious grilled pizza.

DIRECTIONS

1. Preheat a grill to medium-high heat.
2. Combine mushrooms, zucchini, peppers, onion, vinegar, water, 3 teaspoons oil and seasonings in a large mixing bowl.
3. Transfer to grill and cook over medium heat for 10 minutes or until tender, stirring often.
4. Brush crust with remaining oil and spread with pizza sauce.
5. Top evenly with grilled vegetables, tomatoes and cheese.
6. Tent with aluminum foil and grill over medium heat for 5 to 7 minutes or until edges are lightly browned and cheese is melted.
7. Serve warm!

Nutritional Info: Calories: 111, Sodium: 257mg, Dietary Fiber: 1.7g, Fat: 5.4g, Carbs: 12.2g, Protein: 5g.

CORNBREAD WITH JALAPEÑO HONEY BUTTER

SERVINGS: 6

Prep time: 5 minutes
Cook time: 5 minutes

INGREDIENTS

- 1 loaf of cornbread, prepared like Jiffy
- 1/2 cup salted butter, softened
- 1 jalapeno pepper, seeded and minced
- 2 tablespoons raw honey

Hot off the grill this cornbread is delicious and best served alongside your favorite soups or pot of southern style beans. Savory meats spicy sweet for a genuinely delicious flavor combination you're bound to love cooking up.

DIRECTIONS

1. Slice prepared cornbread into squares and split each square horizontally; set aside.
2. Add remaining ingredients to a medium mixing bowl and beat until butter is creamy.
3. Spread the butter on split sides of cornbread squares.
4. Grill cornbread over medium-high heat, about 3 minutes on each side, or until cornbread is crispy and has grill-marks.
5. Serve immediately.

Nutritional Info: Calories: 189, Sodium: 187mg, Dietary Fiber: 0.3g, Fat: 16.4g, Carbs: 10.7g, Protein: 0.9g.

CHARRED BREAD WITH RICOTTA AND CHERRY SALSA

SERVINGS: 6

Prep time: 10 minutes
Cook time: 5 minutes

INGREDIENTS

1 baguette, sliced in half lengthwise

5 tablespoons fresh lemon juice

12 ounces fresh cherries, pitted and cut into 1/3-inch-thick slivers

1/2 cup olive oil, plus more for brushing

12 ounces whole-milk fresh ricotta

Flaky sea salt, for garnish

Ricotta and cherries are the perfect topping for chargrilled bread. Enjoy this bread as an appetizer for a dinner party or the perfect dessert with wine after a romantic dinner.

DIRECTIONS

1. Add lemon juice, cherries, and olive oil to a mixing bowl and toss to coat.
2. Preheat grill to medium-low heat.
3. Brush cut sides of baguette with oil.
4. Grill, cut sides down, until bread is toasted and golden brown, about 3 minutes.
5. Let bread cool for 1 minute, then spread generous amounts of ricotta over both pieces.
6. Cut each half on a diagonal into 6 pieces.
7. Arrange on a plate and top with cherry salsa.
8. Sprinkle lightly with sea salt, and enjoy.

Nutritional Info: Calories: 177, Sodium: 482mg, Dietary Fiber: 1.7g, Fat: 11.9g, Carbs: 12.6g, Protein: 5.5g.

CHAPTER 10
SAUCES AND MARINADES

CLASSIC KANSAS CITY BBQ SAUCE

SERVINGS: 24

Prep time: 10 minutes
Cook time: 15 minutes

INGREDIENTS

1/4 cup yellow onion, finely chopped

2 tablespoons water

2 tablespoons vegetable oil

2 cups ketchup

1/3 cup brown sugar

3 cloves garlic, finely chopped

1 tablespoon apple cider vinegar

1 tablespoon tomato paste

1 tablespoon Worcestershire sauce

1 teaspoon liquid hickory smoke

1 teaspoon ground mustard

Use it on ribs or chicken, or pretty much anything you're cooking on the grill. This classic KC sauce is packed with flavour and great as a marinade or grilling sauce.

DIRECTIONS

1. Place the onion in a food processor and pulse until pureed. Add the water to the onion and pulse few more times.
2. In a medium saucepan, heat the oil and add the onion. When the onion is just starting to soften, add the remaining ingredients and stir well.
3. Stretch or roll dough to a 12-inch circle.
4. Cook the sauce at a simmer for fifteen minutes, stirring occasionally.
5. Remove the pan from the heat and allow to cool for thirty minutes before using or storing in a mason jar.

Nutritional Info: Calories: 799, Sodium: 595mg, Dietary Fiber: 8.6g, Fat: 52.7g, Carbs: 74.9g, Protein: 10g.

SAVORY CHINESE MARINADE

SERVINGS: 1

Prep time: 10 minutes

INGREDIENTS

4 tablespoon low sodium soy sauce

2 tablespoons mirin

2 tablespoon Chinese cooking wine

1 tablespoon corn starch

1 clove garlic, finely chopped

1 teaspoon freshly grated ginger

This authentic Chinese marinade is perfect for chicken, beef, and even veggies. Use it as a marinade and cooking and cooking sauce for barbecuing and stir-frying.

DIRECTIONS

1. To use as a marinade: combine all ingredients in a zipper-lock bag and add your desired meat or vegetables. Allow to marinate for two hours before cooking.

2. To use as a cooking sauce: combine all ingredients in a small bowl and brush onto meat or vegetables as they cook.

Nutritional Info: Calories: 305, Sodium: 221mg, Dietary Fiber: 0.6g, Fat: 14.2g, Carbs: 38.5g, Protein: 3g.

THAI CHILI SAUCE

SERVINGS: 4

Prep time: 10 minutes

INGREDIENTS

- 1 cup water
- 1 cup rice vinegar
- 1 cup sugar
- 2 teaspoons freshly grated ginger
- 1 teaspoon garlic, finely chopped
- 2 teaspoons hot chili pepper, chopped
- 2 teaspoons ketchup
- 2 teaspoons cornstarch

Savory and sweet, this authentic Thai sauce is perfect as a grilling sauce or a finishing sauce. It also makes a perfect dipping sauce.

DIRECTIONS

1. In a medium saucepan, combine the water and vinegar. Bring to a boil and add the sugar, ginger, garlic, chili pepper, and ketchup.
2. Simmer over medium heat for five minutes and then add the corn starch.
3. Remove the pan from the heat and allow to cool completely before using or storing.

Nutritional Info: Calories: 761, Sodium: 54mg, Dietary Fiber: 3.1g, Fat: 36.1g, Carbs: 105.1g, Protein: 3.9g.

CAROLINA GOLD BBQ SAUCE

SERVINGS: 2 CUPS

Prep time: 5 minutes

INGREDIENTS

1 cup yellow mustard

1/2 cup apple cider vinegar

1/4 cup honey

1 tablespoon dark brown sugar

2 teaspoons Worcestershire sauce

1 teaspoon hot sauce

In the Carolinas they prefer their BBQ sauce tangy and sweet. This classic Carolina gold sauce is perfect for grilling or smoking chicken and pork, and best of all, it's so easy to make.

DIRECTIONS

1. In a large bowl combine all ingredients and mix until evenly combined.

Nutritional Info: Calories: 126, Sodium: 97 mg, Dietary Fiber:1.3g, Fat:2.7g, Carbs: 22.8g, Protein: 5. 3g.

JERK RUB

SERVINGS: 1/3 CUPS

Prep time: 5 minutes

INGREDIENTS

2 tablespoons dried onion flakes

1 tablespoon dried thyme

2 teaspoons ground allspice

2 teaspoons black pepper

1/2 teaspoon ground cinnamon

1/2 teaspoon cayenne pepper

1 teaspoon salt

Vegetable oil

Perfect for chicken and pork, this Caribbean rub is perfect for adding just the right amount of herbs and spice.

DIRECTIONS

1. In a small bowl combine the onion, thyme, allspice, pepper, cinnamon, cayenne pepper, and salt. Mix well.
2. To use: coat your meat in oil and then rub a generous amount of spice blend to the meat. Allow to sit for at least one hour before grilling.

Nutritional Info: Calories: 394, Sodium: 2038mg, Dietary Fiber: 0.9g, Fat: 9.6g, Carbs: 75.8g, Protein: 2.4g.

PERUVIAN CHICKEN MARINADE

SERVINGS: 1

Prep Time: 10 minutes

INGREDIENTS

- 3 tablespoons olive oil
- 1/4 cup lime juice
- 4 cloves garlic
- 1 tablespoon salt
- 2 teaspoons paprika
- 1 teaspoon black pepper
- 1 tablespoon ground cumin
- 1 teaspoon dried oregano
- 2 teaspoons sugar

Are you ready for the most flavorful BBQ chicken you've ever had? This South American classic combines rich aromatics and spices for a blend you will want to use every time you cook chicken.

DIRECTIONS

1. In a food processor, combine all ingredients, and pulse until you have a smooth paste.
2. To use: spread the marinade on a whole chicken or chicken pieces. Make sure to work the marinade under the chicken skin for best flavour. Use remaining sauce to baste chicken as you grill.

Nutritional Info: Calories: 101, Sodium: 2mg, Dietary Fiber: 0.7g, Fat: 0.1g, Carbs: 27.2g, Protein: 0.3g.

TERIYAKI SAUCE

SERVINGS: 4

Prep time: 10 minutes
Cook time: 5 minutes

INGREDIENTS

2/3 cup soy sauce

1/4 cup sherry

2 tablespoons sugar

1 teaspoon ground ginger

1 clove garlic, finely chopped

You can make teriyaki with any kind of meat you like, and this sauce works great as both a marinade and a grilling sauce.

DIRECTIONS

1. In a small bowl, combine all ingredients. Stir well and allow to sit at room temperature for an hour before using.

2. To use: place the meat of your choice in a plastic zipper-lock bag. Add half of the teriyaki sauce and allow to marinate for at least one hour and not more than twenty-four hours.

KITCHEN UNIT CONVERSION

1 teaspoon	= 1/3 tbsp	= 4.9 ml
1 dessertspoon	= 2 tsp	= 9.9 ml
1 tablespoon	= 1.5 dstsp / 3 tsp	= 14.8 ml
1 fuid ounce	= 2 tbsp / 6 tsp	= 29.6 ml
1 cup	= 16 tbsp / 48 tsp	= 236.6 ml
1 quart	= 4 cup	= 946 ml
1 gal	= 4 quart / 16 cup	= 3.79 l
1 ounce	= 2 tbsp	= 28.4 g
1 pounds	= 16 oz	= 453.6 g

What's better than a free cookbook?

20 FREE COOKBOOKS!

Finally, a way to get all of the cookbooks you've wanted, for completely free!

HHF Press has published over 100 cookbooks since 2014, and due to new technology we can now give you 20 of our most popular cookbooks for absolutely free!

You'll receive the same well written, professionally designed cookbooks we sell on Amazon, Barnes & Noble and other retailers.

Here are some of the cookbooks included:
Electric Pressure Cooker, Perfect Outdoor Grill, Dutch Oven, Sous Vide, Air Fryer, and many more...

Get them today! No purchase necessary.

Go to: www.HHFPress.com/20/grill

www.ingramcontent.com/pod-product-compliance
Lightning Source LLC
Chambersburg PA
CBHW051803100526
44592CB00016B/2547